CLASSROOM GUIDANCE
GAMES

50 fun, inspirational guidance games; reproducible cards, boards, & worksheets; and letters to parents (PK-6)

by Shannon Trice Black, M.Ed., LPC

youth light
inc.

© 2007, 2005
YouthLight, Inc.
Chapin, SC 29036

Cover Design and Layout by Amy Rule
Project Editing by Susan Bowman

ISBN 1-59850-002-3
EAN 978-1-59850-002-8

Library of Congress Number
2005906227

10 9 8 7 6 5 4 3 2
Printed in the United States

Acknowledgements

First and foremost, I would like to thank the Lord for His wisdom and faithfulness.

A great big thank you to my husband, Gary, for his contributions of fun ideas and explaining the rules of sports to me! Thanks for your patience and putting up with the laptop in the car, at the table, and even in the bed!

Thanks to my daughters, Margaret and Caroline who have had to share so much of their time with my computer! Thanks for making me stop and laugh!

Thank you to Mama, Daddy, Jennifer, and Grandma for believing in me and pushing me to finally do this.

I have to thank my wonderful women's Sunday School class for praying me through this book!

Thanks to Marcy, Kim, Cheryl, Liza, Kay, Kathy, Sarah, and Shannon.

And thanks to the students and staff at Goochland County Public Schools, my old stomping grounds and place of employment, for your support and encouragement.

Introduction

Classroom Guidance Games is composed of fifty games that can be used in grades PK-6. These games focus on bully prevention, social skills, anger management, study skills, emotions, respect, getting along, goal setting, responsibility, careers and self-esteem. This book is designed to be a friendly, easy, fun tool for counselors and teachers to use in the classrooms. Time needed for all games is approximately 30 minutes.

I originally wanted to call this book, "Classroom Guidance Games that Won't Make You or Your Students Want to Throw Up." The book began after I struggled to find activities that students enjoyed learning and did not require hours of preparation. I began making up my own activities that got students out of their seats and engaged their minds, as well as their bodies. Students love to play these games and can learn ways to deal with anger, homework, bullies, safety, goals, friends, and their futures!

I believe that students are better able to learn and retain information if they can move around and engage in fun, challenging activities. Furthermore, I believe that counselors and teachers are more likely to use activities in their classrooms that are easy to assemble and require little preparation. Therefore, this book only contains "tried and true" games that both students and adults will love!

How To Use This Book

Before You Begin

This book is composed of six chapters and divided into two parts. Part I is designed for use in grades PK-2. Part II is designed for use in grades 2-6. During the first half of the school year, games from Part I (PK-2) can be used with 2nd graders. During the second half of the school year, games from Part II (2-6) can be used with 2nd graders. Part I and Part II are each divided into the following three chapters:

Respect: Games in the Respect sections concentrate on anti-bullying, getting along with others, conflict resolution, tattling, teamwork, and safety.

Reflection: Games in the Reflection sections concentrate on self-esteem, positive communication, understanding and communicating feelings, anger control, and social skills.

Responsibility: Games in the Responsibility sections concentrate on goal setting, study skills, and career information.

How to Play

The required materials are listed for each game. Most materials are simple household items and should be easy to obtain. Game set-up is designed to be quick and easy. Pre-Game Directions include questions and discussion to help prepare students for the game. The Follow-Up sections include additional activities, game variations, and discussion questions which can be done immediately following the game or at a later date.

Time Needed

Each game is designed to last approximately 30 minutes.

Warm-Ups

I suggest doing a warm-up activity such as a simple stretch or a few jumping jacks. Sometimes, I even throw in a yoga or a dance move! Warm-ups help students transition from their previous activities to the classroom guidance lesson. It can also be helpful for you and meaningful to students if you practice everyone's names before beginning the lesson.

Classroom Control

Due to the energetic, competitive nature of games, it can be challenging to maintain classroom control. I have found that starting the game with a bank of a few points and deducting points or skipping a team's turn for loud, unruly, or unsportsmanlike behaviors helps keep the volume down and the attitudes positive.

Rewards

I have not found it to be beneficial to give rewards to the winning teams. I believe that too much emphasis on the "winners" takes away from the fun and the teaching of the games. At the end of a game, I usually tell the winning team to give themselves a silent hurrah. I usually tell the teams that did not win to give themselves a pat on the back. I spend very little time focusing on the actual winner of the game. However, I do believe that it is important to emphasize good sportsmanship in the games. Small tokens, stickers, or candy can be given to all students who work hard, work together, and are supportive of their classmates.

Letters to Parents/Guardians

This book contains a letter to parents or guardians about each of the fifty games. After completing a classroom guidance lesson, the letter can be sent home with the students. The letters provide parents/guardians with a brief summary of the classroom guidance game as well as tips on how to encourage their children at home.

Table of Contents

Table of Contents

Table of Contents

Chapter One

Respect

Games in this chapter concentrate on anti-bullying, getting along with others, conflict resolution, tattling, teamwork, and safety for grades PK-2.

Game #1

Grade Levels

PK - 2

Materials

• Copies of the Smiley Face/Sad Face Sheet (pg. 14)

• Copies of the Scenario Cards (pp. 12-13)

• Scarf or Handkerchief for Blindfolding

• Tape

Time Needed

Approximately 30 minutes

Skills Covered

• Tattling

• Respect for Others

Pin the Face on the Tattletale

Introduction

This game is a take-off from the birthday party favorite "Pin the Tail on the Donkey." Kids love the fun of being blindfolded and playing the game while learning the difference between "tattling" and "telling."

Pre-Game Directions

1. Cut out the faces and the Scenario Cards.

2. Explain to students the difference between telling and tattling. People need to "tell" adults if someone is being dangerous, stealing, threatening someone, or hurting someone. "Tattling" is when people tell an adult what someone else is doing, usually with the intention of getting someone else in trouble.

3. Explain that respectful students have respect for their teachers, parents, friends, and family. Respectful people tell adults if someone is being dangerous, stealing, threatening someone or hurting someone. Respectful people do not tattle. Tattling is disrespectful because it takes time away from everyone's learning and it is used to try to get others in trouble.

4. Draw a person on the board or on a large piece of butcher paper. Leave the face blank – don't draw eyes, nose, mouth, etc.

5. Show the students the cutouts of the smiley faces and the sad faces. Show the students the smiling faces and explain how "telling" situations make students and adults happy because the adults are able to help the students from being hurt. Show the students the sad faces and explain how "tattling" situations make adults and students sad because they take time away from learning and they cause others to get in trouble.

6. Go over a few examples with the students such as – "Dasheem told his teacher that Sally was scribbling all over her paper." "Is this telling or tattling?" "How do you think this made the teacher and students feel?" "It probably made them feel sad because their teacher had to stop teaching and listen to Dasheem tattling." Put a piece of tape on a sad face and place it on the person drawn on board for an example of tattling. For an example of telling, you can use an example such as – "Kara told her mom that a boy on the bus has been pinching her." "Is this an example of tattling or telling?" "Kara's mom was probably very proud and happy that Kara was brave enough to tell her. Now Kara's mom will be able to talk to someone at the school to make sure that the boy will not pinch her anymore." Put a piece of tape on the happy face and place that on the person drawn on the board.

Pin the Face
on the Tattletale

Grade Levels

PK - 2

Game Directions

1. Allow each student to pick a scenario card that depicts either a telling or a tattling scenario. Each student will decide if he/she thinks the situation is telling or tattling. If the student answers correctly, he/she will get to choose a smiley face (for the telling situations) or a sad face (for the tattling situations).

2. Place a piece of tape on the chosen smiley or sad face.

3. Blindfold the student and instruct him/her to place the face on the person drawn on the board.

4. Play as time allows. Make sure each student gets at least one turn to put a face on the person.

Materials

- Copies of the Smiley Face/Sad Face Sheet (pg.14)
- Copies of the Scenario Cards (pp.12-13)
- Scarf or Handkerchief for Blindfolding
- Tape

Time Needed

Approximately 30 minutes

Skills Covered

- Tattling
- Respect for Others

Follow-Up

- Why do you think it is important to not tattle? Why do you think it is important to tell an adult if someone is in danger of being hurt?
- What can you do to make sure that you do a good job of not tattling? What can you do to make sure that you do a good job of telling an adult if someone is in danger of being hurt?
- Describe a day in your classroom where nobody told on anyone else. How do you think the students would feel towards each other? How do you think your teacher would feel? Do you think that you would learn more on that day of school?

Pin the Face on the Tattletale Scenario Cards

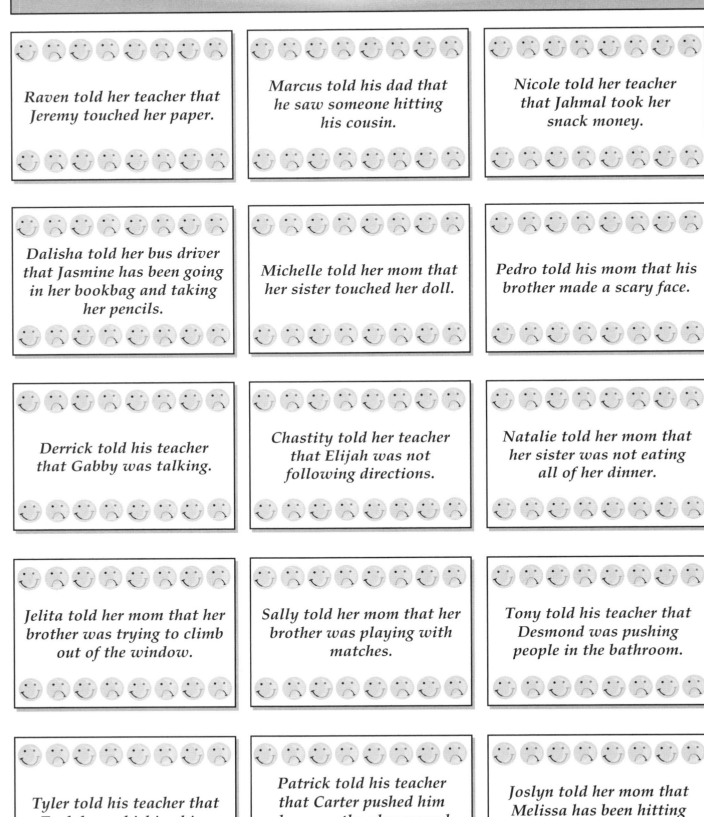

Raven told her teacher that Jeremy touched her paper.

Marcus told his dad that he saw someone hitting his cousin.

Nicole told her teacher that Jahmal took her snack money.

Dalisha told her bus driver that Jasmine has been going in her bookbag and taking her pencils.

Michelle told her mom that her sister touched her doll.

Pedro told his mom that his brother made a scary face.

Derrick told his teacher that Gabby was talking.

Chastity told her teacher that Elijah was not following directions.

Natalie told her mom that her sister was not eating all of her dinner.

Jelita told her mom that her brother was trying to climb out of the window.

Sally told her mom that her brother was playing with matches.

Tony told his teacher that Desmond was pushing people in the bathroom.

Tyler told his teacher that Zach keeps kicking him.

Patrick told his teacher that Carter pushed him down on the playground and kicked him.

Joslyn told her mom that Melissa has been hitting her and threatening her.

Pin the Face on the Tattletale Scenario Cards

Danielle told her teacher that Odell was using his blue crayon instead of the red one.

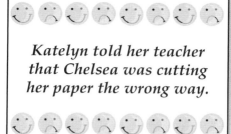

Katelyn told her teacher that Chelsea was cutting her paper the wrong way.

Monique told her teacher that Tiffany took her lunch money.

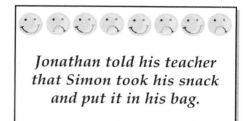

Monique told her teacher that someone has been hitting her brother.

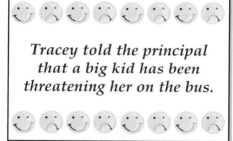

Savannah told her dad that her sister was riding her bike in the road.

Kirsten told her teacher that Shawn was not reading his book.

Jonathan told his teacher that Simon took his snack and put it in his bag.

Tracey told the principal that a big kid has been threatening her on the bus.

Jeffrey told his teacher that Alex rolled his eyes at him.

Ashley told her mom that her sister was touching her game.

Lachelle told her teacher that Melanie was sticking out her tongue.

Tara told her teacher that Henry was talking to someone.

James told his teacher that Quincy was not doing his work.

Teresa told her teacher that Kelly was pushing people out of the swings.

Leah told her dad that her friend, Sophie, broke a lamp in the house.

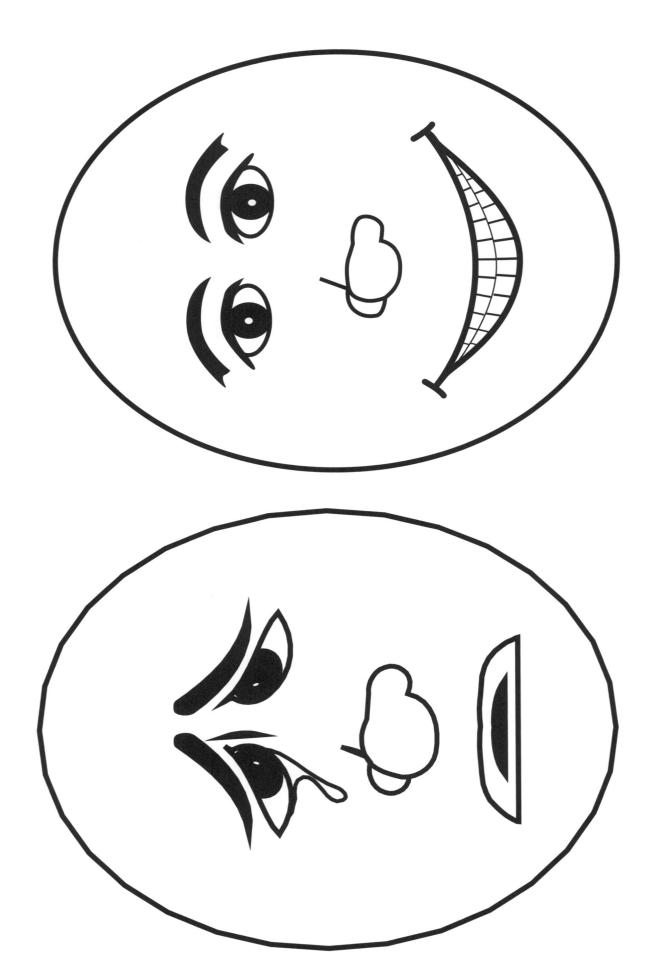

Dear Parents/Guardians,

Today, your child participated in a classroom guidance game entitled, "Pin the Face on the Tattletale." The objective of this game was to teach students the difference between tattling on others and telling an adult when someone needs help. We talked about how tattling is usually used to get someone else in trouble. We discussed the difference between tattling and telling an adult when someone is being hurt or threatened. We talked about how it is important to tell adults when we need help, but unnecessary to tattle on others.

In this game, students were given scenarios. Students had to determine whether the scenario was a tattling situation or a telling situation. Students taped smiley faces on the board for telling situations and sad faces on the board for tattling situations. The most fun part was that students were blindfolded while taping the faces on the board!

At home tonight, please remind your child of the difference between tattling and telling. You can even play a round or two of "Pin the Face on the Tattletale!"

Thanks for your support,

Game #2

Grade Levels

PK - 2

Materials

• Paper Bag
• Small Slips of Paper

Time Needed

Approximately 30 minutes

Skills Covered

• Respecting Differences

Guess Who I Am!

Introduction

This game helps students learn about each other and helps them to respect one another's differences.

Pre-Game Directions

1. Talk to the students about how we are all different. Talk about how our differences are the things that make us really cool. Sometimes people may not respect our differences, but we need to be proud of our differences and respectful of others. These differences are what make us the individual, talented people that we all are.

2. Tell the students something about you that is different that makes you really great. For example, I usually talk about my big feet. When I was in school, I was teased about my really big feet. However, my feet are wonderful because they help me run fast!

3. Tell the students to close their eyes and think of something really cool about themselves.

Game Directions

1. Give each student a slip of paper.

2. Tell the students to write down something cool about themselves on the slips of paper. Tell them not to tell anyone and not to put their names on the paper.

3. Ask the students to fold their paper after they are finished writing.

4. Collect all the papers in the paper bag.

5. Let each student pick a paper out of the bag. Read it and give the students three guesses to figure out whose paper it is.

6. Repeat #5 until all papers have been read.

Follow-Up

• What is the coolest thing you learned about someone else today?
• What is something that people sometimes tease you about that makes you unique and special?
• How do you think the world would be if we all were exactly the same and we did not have any "cool" or unique characteristics?

Dear Parents/Guardians,

Today, your child participated in a classroom guidance game entitled, "Guess Who I Am." The objective of this game was to encourage students to learn more about each other and to respect one another's differences. We talked about how we need to be proud of our differences and we need to be respectful of others. We talked about how our differences make us unique, talented individuals.

In this game, students wrote down the coolest things about themselves on slips of paper. The papers were read to the class and students had to guess who wrote them. This game revealed many talents and interests.

At home tonight, you can encourage your child to talk about the coolest things he/she discovered about his/her class. Try to guess what your child shared about him/herself. Encourage your family members to share their individual strengths with each other.

Thanks for your support,

Game #3

Materials
• Two Pieces of Rope
• Cassette or CD Player
• Musical CD or Cassette

Time Needed
Approximately 30 minutes

Skills Covered
• Working Together
• Respect for Others

Musical Teamwork

Introduction
This game is similar to the game "Musical Chairs," except that a piece of rope is used instead of chairs and students actually try to keep everyone "in" as the space gets smaller. This game helps students practice respectful behaviors by working together to include everyone.

Pre-Game Directions
1. Talk to the students about the importance of including everyone. Explain to them that this is "their" class and "their" school. All students have the job of being respectful and including everyone.

2. Ask students if they have ever not been included in an activity. Ask them how it feels to be left out of something they would like to do.

3. Tell the students that we will be playing a game where they will need to make sure that they include everyone.

4. Show the students the pieces of rope. Tell them that when the music stops, their team will need to try to fit inside a circle made of the rope. It is each team's responsibility to include everyone. Teams that are not respectful of one another and blame each other will lose points.

Game Directions
1. Divide the class into two teams.

2. Use the pieces of rope to make two large circles that the students can easily fit inside.

3. Begin playing the music. Instruct the students to walk around the outside of the circles as the music plays.

4. Stop the music. Instruct the teams to quickly get all students inside the circle. The first team to get all team members inside the circle and to stay inside it for five seconds wins 5 points.

5. Continue the game by repeating #3 and #4, but make the circles smaller each time so that it becomes much more difficult to get everyone inside the circle and to stay inside it for five seconds.

Game Tips
• In order to keep this game from getting too wild, you can take off points for things like screaming or even falling.
• If the circles become too small too quickly, feel free to make them bigger again, or even change the shapes to ovals, triangles, rectangles, etc.

Musical Teamwork

Game Tips continued...

- Praise the teams for respectful teamwork. Point out that the teams that are working together are quieter and are falling less than the teams that are not working together.

Follow-Up

- How did you feel when you were trying to stay inside the circle?
- How did your team work together to keep everyone inside the circle?
- What can you do at home and at school to make sure that you include everyone and work as a team?

Grade Levels
PK - 2

Materials
- Two Pieces of Rope
- Cassette or CD Player
- Musical CD or Cassette

Time Needed
Approximately 30 minutes

Skills Covered
- Working Together
- Respect for Others

Dear Parents/Guardians,

Today, your child participated in a classroom guidance game entitled, "Musical Teamwork." The objective of this game was to teach students how to include everyone. We talked about how it feels to be left out of an activity or left out of a group. We discussed the importance of reaching out to others to make sure that we do not exclude others.

Similar to "Musical Chairs," this game involved students walking around while music played. However, unlike Musical Chairs, the object of this game was to make sure that everyone had a place once the music stopped. Teams competed against each other to see who could work together to fit their team in the smallest space.

At home tonight, you can encourage your child to talk about ways that he/she can include everyone at school and at home.

Thanks for your support,

Safety Soccer

Game #4

Grade Levels
PK - 2

Materials
- Copy of Soccer Field Game Board (pg. 23)
- Copy of Soccer Goal (pg.24)
- Copy of Two Soccer Balls (pg.23)
- Copies of Safety Question Cards (pp.25-26)
- Soccer Ball / Other Type of Ball
- Tape

Time Needed
Approximately 30 minutes

Skills Covered
- Safety for Self and Others

Introduction

This game is a great indoor game of soccer that teaches the importance of safety. Safe behaviors are a way for people to show respect to themselves and to others.

Pre-Game Directions

1. Cut out two soccer balls on soccer field game board. Place a piece of tape on the back of each paper soccer ball.

2. Tape copy of soccer field on chalkboard.

3. Tape copy of goal sheet on bottom of wall or classroom door.

4. Talk to the students about the importance of safety. Explain that safety is a very important way to show respect because it protects people and property.

5. Ask students to say their favorite safety rules in the classroom, on the bus, in the cafeteria, on the playground, at home, etc.

6. Explain that you will be playing a game of soccer where students can practice important safety rules.

Game Directions

1. Divide class into two teams – the Lightning Bolts and the Shining Stars.

2. Tape the lightning bolt soccer ball on the lightning bolt player marked "1." Tape the shining star soccer ball on the shining star player marked "1."

3. First student from the Lighting Bolt team draws a card. If the student answers safety question correctly, the Lightning Bolt team can move their soccer ball the number of passes marked on the card. For example, if the card states "3 passes," the soccer ball will be moved from player #1 to player #4.

4. Next, the Shining Stars team proceeds in same manner as the Lightning Bolt team.

5. The first team to reach the goal (next pass after reaching player #10) gets one point. The team gets an opportunity to get an extra point by having one student (lightly) kick the soccer ball and hit the paper soccer goal taped on wall.

6. Both teams return the paper soccer balls to player #1. The team that did not get the last goal gets to go first. The game continues as described in #3.

Game #4

Grade Levels

PK - 2

Materials

- Copy of Soccer Field Game Board (pg. 23)
- Copy of Soccer Goal (pg.24)
- Copy of Two Soccer Balls (pg.23)
- Copies of Safety Question Cards (pp.25-26)
- Soccer Ball / Other Type of Ball
- Tape

Time Needed

Approximately 30 minutes

Skills Covered

- Safety for Self and Others

Safety Soccer

Game Directions continued...

7. At the end of time allotted for game, the team with most points wins the game of Safety Soccer!

Follow-Up

- What do you think is the most important rule at school? Why do you think this is the most important rule?
- Why do you think it is important for everyone to obey safety rules all the time? What could happen if just a few people decided to break some rules?
- What do you think is the hardest rule to obey at school? Why is it still important to obey this rule?

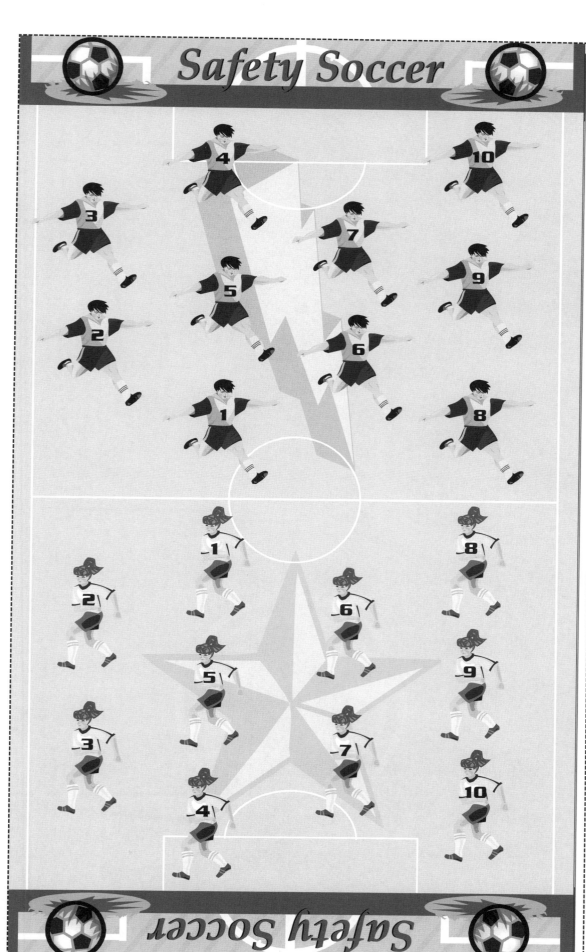

Safety Soccer

Cut along dotted lines.

Safety Soccer Cards

Who should you call if your mom has gotten very sick and cannot use the phone?

1 Pass

What should you do if you see medicine on the floor in your bathroom at home?

2 Passes

Should you let your baby brothers, sisters, and cousins put money in their mouths?

3 Passes

What three numbers do you push on your phone to call for emergency help?

1 Pass

Should you play with matches?

2 Passes

What should you do if your sister is playing with a lighter?

3 Passes

Should you cross a road by yourself?

1 Pass

What should you do if your clothes are on fire?

2 Passes

What should you do if your house is on fire?

3 Passes

Should you get in a car with someone you don't know?

1 Pass

Should you run around with scissors?

2 Passes

Should you use your oven at home without the help of an adult?

3 Passes

Should you ride your bike near the road?

1 Pass

What should you do if you see a gun?

2 Passes

Should you touch or put anything in an electric socket?

3 Passes

Should you go outside without asking your parents?

1 Pass

Should you talk to someone you do not know?

2 Passes

Should you walk away from your parents in a store?

3 Passes

Safety Soccer Cards

Should you let your baby sisters, brothers, or cousins play on or near the stairs?

1 Pass

Should you walk with an adult in a parking lot?

2 Passes

Should you run in a parking lot?

3 Passes

What should you do if your cousin is playing with cigarettes?

1 Pass

What should you do if you see broken glass or nails on the ground?

2 Passes

Where should all medicine be kept in your house?

3 Passes

Is it ever okay to take medicine without a grownup helping you?

1 Pass

What is your phone number?

2 Passes

What is your first and last name?

3 Passes

If you ever get separated or lost from your parents in a store, what should you do?

1 Pass

Should you ever hide from your parents in a store?

2 Passes

What should you do for safety when you first get in a car?

3 Passes

What should you always wear when you are riding a bike?

1 Pass

Is it okay to play with knives in your kitchen?

2 Passes

How should you act during a school fire drill?

3 Passes

Should you take any food from someone you do not know?

1 Pass

Should you get in a pool without a grownup with you?

2 Passes

Who should you ask for help if you are ever lost?

3 Passes

Dear Parents/Guardians,

Today, your child participated in a classroom guidance game entitled, "Safety Soccer." The objective of this game was to teach students the importance of safety. We talked about how safety is an important way to show respect because it protects people and our environment.

In this game, students competed against each other on teams. Players picked cards with safety questions. If correctly answered, teams were able to pass the soccer ball (on our soccer field game board) one to three times. Each time the ball reached the goal, the team scored a point.

At home tonight, you can review some of your family rules of safety with your child.

Thanks for you support,

Game #5

Grade Levels

PK - 2

Materials

- Markers
- Copies of Bullying Cards (pp.30-31)
- Large Sheet of Paper

Time Needed

Approximately 30 minutes

Skills Covered

- No-Bullying Behaviors
- Respect for Self and Others

No-Bullying Square Game

Introduction

This game is a fun, easy way to teach and reinforce respectful behaviors that discourage bullying behaviors. Teams compete against one another by correctly answering anti-bullying questions and connecting two dots on the "Make A Square" paper. Each time a team player connects the last two dots of a square, his/her team gets one point. The team with the most completed squares wins the game.

Pre-Game Directions

1. Copy bullying cards.

2. On a large sheet of paper, write "MAKE A SQUARE" in large letters across the top.

3. Below the "MAKE A SQUARE" title, draw 25 dots, 5 rows across and 5 rows down.

4. Hang the "Make a Square" paper in front of the classroom.

5. Help students define "bullying." Explain that bullying behaviors are those that have the potential to harm others physically or mentally. Discuss the importance of engaging in behaviors that do not encourage bullying.

6. Divide class into two teams.

7. Explain that in Round One, each team will get a chance to define bullying or a bullying behavior. If answered correctly, the team will get to connect two of the dots on the paper. After Round One, teams will pick bullying cards. If answered correctly, teams will get to connect two dots on the paper. Teams compete against each other to complete a square on the "Make a Square" sheet! Each time a team connects the last two dots on a square, that team receives a point.

Game Directions

1. In Round One, player from Team A defines "bullying" or an example of a bullying behavior. If answered correctly, player connects two dots on the "Make a Square" paper.

2. Player from Team B proceeds as in #1.

3. Repeat steps #1 and #2 until all players have connected two dots.

4. After all players have connected two dots, begin Round Two.

5. In Round Two, player from Team A picks a bullying card. If answered correctly, player connects two dots on the "Make a Square" paper.

No-Bullying Square Game

Game Directions continued...

6. Player from Team B proceeds as Team A.

7. Repeat steps #5 and #6 for the rest of the game.

8. Each time a team completes the last two dots on a square, that team puts the letter for their team (A or B) inside the completed square and receives a point.

9. Play as time allows. The team with the most points wins the game.

Follow-Up

- How do you think people feel when they are being bullied?
- Why is important to tell an adult if someone is being bullied? Why do you think people are sometimes afraid to tell if they are being bullied?
- How can you make sure that you always include others and that you act respectful towards everyone?

Game #5

Grade Levels
PK - 2

Materials
- Markers
- Copies of Bullying Cards (pp.30-31)
- Large Sheet of Paper

Time Needed
Approximately 30 minutes

Skills Covered
- No-Bullying Behaviors
- Respect for Self and Others

No-Bullying Square Game Cards

Your friend, Sammy, is visiting you at your house. Should you tell Sammy not to touch your toys and games? What should you do with your toys and games?

Kari trips and drops her books. What should you do?

Jose keeps hitting Latrice when the teacher is not looking. What should you do?

Antonio threatened to beat you up in the hallway. What should you do?

Sarah is a new student at your school. What are some respectful things you can do to make her feel welcome?

Jorge does not have anyone to play with at recess. What can you do to help him have fun?

Jasmine is sad. What are some things you can say to make her feel better?

Rodney is crying at recess. What are some things you can do and say in order to help him?

Keisha cannot find her pencil and you have an extra one. What could you do to help?

Chuck fell down and ripped his pants. If everyone else laughs, should you laugh? What could you say to help him feel better?

Everyone is making fun of Maria's new shoes. What should you do? What can you say or do to help Maria feel better?

Every day on the bus Jermaine pokes you in the back of your neck with a pencil. When you ask him to stop, he keeps doing it. What should you do?

Juan said that he is going to bring his baseball bat to school to beat up Tony. What should you do or say?

Olivia said that, if you sit beside Krista, no one else will be your friend. What should you do?

Every day, Raoul begs you to give him your snack money. Even when you tell him, "No," he will not stop asking. What should you do?

No-Bullying Square Game Cards

Alicia said that if you do not give her your lunch money, she is going to beat up your little sister. What should you do?

Todd took your game from you on the bus. He will not give it back and said that he will beat you up if you tell on him. What should you do?

Georgia is your best friend and she is very nice to you. However, she told you that if you are friends with Rochelle, she will not be your friend anymore. What should you do?

Your friend, Ophelia, has a club and she says that Annie cannot be in the club. What should you do or say?

Monica said that if you invite Helena to your birthday party, she will not come. Should you still invite Helena? What should you do or say?

Keiko and Phoebe are sitting with you at lunch. Keiko wants to tell you a secret, but she says that Phoebe cannot hear it. What should you do or say?

Terrell tripped and fell down the stairs. Everyone is laughing at him. What should you do?

Greg got new glasses. The other students are calling him names. What is something you could say to Greg to make him feel better?

Quinton pushed Billy off the swings. What should you do or say?

Tremaine said that in order to be in his club, you have to steal something from the teacher's desk. What should you do?

Garrett took some money from the teacher's desk. He threatened to beat up anyone who tells on him. What should you do or say?

No one ever picks Mario to be on their kickball team and they yell, "Don't pick Mario!" Mario really wants to play. What should you do?

Latisha has her head down on her desk and is not talking to anyone. What could you say or do to help find out if she is okay?

Sachi said that only popular girls can be in her club. What should you do or say?

J.B. keeps calling Owen, "Fat Boy" and everyone laughs. What should you do or say?

Dear Parents/Guardians,

Today, your child participated in a classroom guidance game entitled, "No-Bullying Square Game." The objective of this game was to teach students the importance of engaging in behaviors that do not encourage bullying. We defined bullying and discussed the importance of telling an adult if someone is being bullied.

In this game, students were divided into two teams. Teams competed against one another to connect lines in order to complete a square on a large matrix of dots. Each player was given the opportunity to answer questions about bullying and appropriate behaviors. If answered correctly, players were able to connect two of the dots on the matrix of dots. Each time a team completed a square, the team received one point.

At home tonight, you can emphasize the importance of your child telling adults if he/she is bullied. You can also encourage your child to continue to engage in behaviors that encourage everyone to get along.

Thanks for your support,

Sticks and Stones

Grade
PK - 2

Materi.
- Small ~~~ ...ge & Stones
- Copies of the "Sticks & Stones" Cards (pp.35-36)
- Small Pile of Shredded Newspapers & Magazines

Time Needed
Approximately 30 minutes

Skills Covered
- Tattling
- Respect for Self and Others

Introduction

This game is taken from the old phrase, "Sticks and stones may break my bones, but words will never harm me." It is very easy to play and students get a big kick out of the visuals of the sticks, stones, and words! This game emphasizes the difference between behaviors that hurt and behaviors that can be ignored.

Pre-Game Directions

1. Copy and cut out "Sticks and Stones" cards.

2. Place a pile of shredded newspapers and magazines in front of the classroom. This pile is the "words" pile.

3. Place a pile of sticks and stones in front of the classroom.

4. Explain to students that you will be a playing a game that emphasizes the difference between behaviors that hurt and behaviors that can be ignored.

5. Ask the class if they have heard the phrase, "Sticks and stones may break my bones, but words will never harm me."

6. Ask the class what they think this phrase means. Explain to them that behaviors that hurt (like sticks and stones can hurt) are those in which we need to have an adult help us. Behaviors that are just words can usually be ignored.

7. Show the students the pile of sticks and stones and the pile of magazines and newspapers (the words) in front of the classroom.

8. Explain to the class that they will each get a turn to pick a question card. Each student will need to decide if the behavior described on the card is one that could hurt or one that could be ignored. If it is one that hurts, the student needs to drop the card on the pile of sticks and stones. If the behavior is one that can be ignored, the student needs to drop the card on the pile of words (the shredded magazines and newspapers).

9. Give the students a few examples of behaviors and have them try to figure out if they are behaviors that could hurt (like sticks and stones) or could be ignored (like words). You can give an example such as, "If someone hits you, is this a behavior that hurts or can be ignored?" Explain to the class that this behavior card would go on top of the pile of sticks and stones because it hurts. Give another example such as, "Someone calls you a name." Explain to the class that this card would go on top of the pile of words because it is full of words that can be ignored.

Game #6

Grade Levels
PK - 2

Materials
- Small Pile of Twigs & Stones
- Copies of the "Sticks & Stones" Cards (pp.35-36)
- Small Pile of Shredded Newspapers & Magazines

Time Needed
Approximately 30 minutes

Skills Covered
- Tattling
- Respect for Self and Others

Sticks and Stones

Game Directions

1. Student picks a Sticks and Stones Card.

2. Read the card to the student.

3. Student must decide if this card goes in the pile of sticks and stones or in the pile of words.

4. Next student picks a card.

5. Repeat steps #2 and #3.

6. Game continues in same manner until all students have had a turn.

Follow-Up

- What are some things that your friends sometimes do that you could choose to ignore?
- Why do you think it is important to ignore things that people do that bother us but do not hurt us?
- How should you act to make sure that you do not do things that hurt or bother other people?

Sticks and Stones Cards

Kyle calls you "Fat Head."

Rosalie pushes you off the monkey bars.

Tammy pulls your hair.

Jennifer calls you "Big Foot."

Carlos says your hair looks funny.

Cindy laughs at you when you trip getting on the bus.

Jessie calls you "Stupid Mouth."

Teresa says you look like a monkey.

Patty keeps kicking you.

Laura always sticks out her foot and trips you on the bus.

Rosia says you look ugly.

Raymond makes fun of your sweater.

Marissa makes fun of your sister.

Felicia makes fun of your shoes.

Carmen says no one wants to be your friend.

Sticks and Stones Cards

Kayla says you cannot play with her.

Salome shoves you down the stairs.

Tess threatens to stab you in your arm with her scissors.

Amber pushes you out of your desk.

Victor hits you in the head with his book three times.

Megan pushes you into the lunch table.

Shoshanna pokes you with her pencil.

Julio pushes you off the swings.

Kelly calls you "Fatty."

Zoe says you are a baby and need to stay home with your mom.

Tyson says you look like a pig.

Raymond shoves you against the wall.

Missy scratches you across your face.

Marguerite calls you "Ugly Face."

Phillip threatens to punch you in the nose.

Dear Parents/Guardians,

Today, your child participated in a classroom guidance game entitled, "Sticks and Stones." The objective of this game was to teach students the difference between behaviors that hurt and behaviors that can be ignored. We talked about the old saying, "Sticks and stones may break my bones, but words will never harm me." We talked about how mean words can often be ignored.

In this game, students picked cards that described situations that hurt (physically) or could be ignored (words). Students had to place their cards on a pile of sticks and stones if the behaviors could physically hurt or on a pile of shredded newspaper if the behaviors could be ignored (words).

At home tonight, encourage your child to talk about the importance of ignoring mean words, even when our feelings are hurt.

Thanks for your support,

Grade Levels
PK - 2

Materials
• None

Time Needed
Approximately 30 minutes

Skills Covered
• Safety for Self and Others

Safety Stand-Up

Introduction

This game is very similar to "Simon Says." Students have a great time demonstrating their knowledge of safe behaviors!

Pre-Game Directions

1. Discuss the importance of safety with the class. Ask them questions such as:
   • "Why is it important to be safe at school?"
   • "Why is it important to be safe at home?"
   • "Why is it important to be safe on the bus?"

2. Ask the students if they are familiar with the game, "Simon Says." Take a few minutes to review the game of "Simon Says" with the students. For example, say "Simon says touch your nose" (students touch their noses). Next, say "touch your feet" (students should not touch their feet).

3. Explain that the class will be playing a game similar to "Simon Says." In this game, they will need to listen carefully to the safety scenarios read to them. If the scenario is safe, the students will need to follow the instruction given for a safe behavior. If the scenario is not safe, the students will need to follow the instruction given for the unsafe behavior.

4. Give the students example scenarios such as, "Billy does not run in the hallway" - students should stand up because this behavior is safe. Another example is, "Sarah stands up while the bus is moving" – students should remain sitting.

Game Directions

1. Read the scenario instructions to students.

2. Read the 7 "Safety Stand-Up Scenarios" for each set of instructions.

Follow-Up

• How do you think a safe person acts on the bus?
• How do you think a safe person acts at school?
• How do you think a safe person acts at home?

Safety Stand-Up Scenarios

Safe Behavior

Stand Up

Unsafe Behavior

Stay Sitting

Instruct students to stand up if a behavior is safe or stay sitting if the behavior is unsafe.

1. Devonte is yelling on the bus.
2. Patty is listening to her teacher.
3. Colby is spitting water in the hallway.
4. Jamie is sitting in her seat on the bus.
5. Kara is following her teacher's directions.
6. Graham is playing with knives in his mom's kitchen.
7. Sharonda is putting batteries in her mouth.

Safe Behavior

Stand Up

Unsafe Behavior

Touch Your Toes

Instruct students to stand up if a behavior is safe or touch their toes if the behavior is unsafe.

1. Tyrone is playing with the oven in his house without his mom helping him.
2. Damian is listening to his mom.
3. Terry is wearing a helmet when she rides her bike.
4. Jimmy is throwing food in the cafeteria.
5. Todd is doing exactly what his dad asks him to do.
6. Jeffrey is playing in the road.
7. Marcus is pushing people off the playground equipment.

Safe Behavior

Touch Your Nose

Unsafe Behavior

Touch Your Knees

Instruct students to touch their noses if a behavior is safe or touch their knees if the behavior is unsafe.

1. Jennifer is having good manners in the cafeteria.
2. Sherry is waiting patiently for her turn on the swings.
3. Jeremy is throwing water and toilet paper in the school bathroom.
4. April is playing with matches at her house.
5. Gloria picks up small toys and money so that her little sister cannot put them in her mouth.
6. Anita makes sure that the area around her desk is clean so that no one will trip over her things.
7. Jermaine keeps his eyes on his teacher when his teacher is talking.

Safety Stand-Up Scenarios

Safe Behavior

Stand On One Leg

Unsafe Behavior

Touch Your Chin

Instruct students to stand on one leg if a behavior is safe or touch their chins if the behavior is unsafe.

1. Margaret makes sure that she listens to and reads all directions before beginning her work.
2. Tory plays with his dad's pocketknife.
3. Perry knows how to call 911 in case of an emergency.
4. Donnie throws balls inside the house.
5. Dominique saw some broken glass in her backyard and immediately told her mom about it.
6. Cindy never talks to strangers.
7. Sebastian knows his full name, his address and his phone number.

Safe Behavior

Jump

Unsafe Behavior

Dance

Instruct students to jump if a behavior is safe or dance if the behavior is unsafe.

1. Caroline always stays beside her mom in the store.
2. Mitchell has matches in his pocket at school.
3. Grace walks away from her mom in the mall if she sees something she wants to buy.
4. Yolanda plays with her mom's keys in her mom's car.
5. Calvin wears kneepads and a helmet when he skateboards.
6. Devon does not leave his backyard without his parents' permission.
7. Lionel only runs and throws balls outside.

Safe Behavior

Hands in the Air

Unsafe Behavior

Hands On Your Hips

Instruct students to touch their noses if a behavior is safe or touch their knees if the behavior is unsafe.

1. Ricardo follows the directions given by his bus driver.
2. Millie plays with her dad's medicine.
3. Angie runs with scissors in her hands.
4. Jaynie squirts her glue in other students' faces.
5. Meg wears kneepads and a helmet when skating or rollerblading.
6. Vinny waits patiently for his turn on the monkey bars.
7. Lamont never tries to butt in front of others in the cafeteria line.

Dear Parents/Guardians,

Today, your child participated in a classroom guidance game entitled, "Safety Stand-Up." The objective of this game was to teach students the importance of obeying rules of safety at school and at home. We talked about rules of safety at school and at home that are for our protection.

In this game, behaviors were described to the class. Students had to follow certain directions if the described behavior was safe and certain directions if the described behavior was unsafe. For example, students had to stand up if the behavior was safe and touch their toes if the behavior was unsafe.

At home tonight, you can emphasize the importance of obeying safety rules at home and at school. You can explain that these rules protect people from harm.

Thanks for your support,

Game #8

Grade Levels

PK - 2

Materials

• Approximately 200 Blocks
(you can use different kinds & sizes)

Time Needed

Approximately 30 minutes

Skills Covered

• Working Together

• Respect for Others

Teamwork Towers

Introduction

Students are given a great chance to work on respectful ways to work together as a team. It can be very frustrating for students to work together in a group or on a team.

Pre-Game Directions

1. Ask students if they have ever had to work with a group of people on an assignment, a project, or on a sports team.

2. Ask the students questions such as:
   • "Do you think it is difficult to work with others sometimes?" "Why or why not?"
   • "Why is it important that we work together?"
   • "What would happen if a soccer team did not work together but just argued with each other – do you think they would win any games?"

3. Explain to the students that they will be racing against each other to build a tall tower of blocks. Each team will begin the game with ten points. Every time you hear disrespectful comments or see behaviors that do not exhibit good sportsmanship, you will deduct one point from that team.

4. Divide the students into groups of 3-5 students.

5. First team-building event - each group must pick a name for their team. They have one minute to respectfully pick this name.

Game Directions

1. Divide up the blocks evenly between the teams.

2. Tell the students that they have three minutes to build a tower. The team that builds the tallest tower will receive five points.

3. Remind the teams that points will be deducted for disrespectful comments or behaviors.

4. Start timing for 3 minutes. Award five points to the winning team.

5. Continue playing the game as time allows.

Follow-Up

• What things did your team do to help build a tall tower?
• How do you think a great baseball team wins a game? What are some things they need to do together to play a great game?
• What are some games and activities in which you participate that require teamwork? Why is it important for your team to use good teamwork?

Dear Parents/Guardians,

Today, your child participated in a classroom guidance game entitled, "Teamwork Towers." The objective of this game was to encourage students to work together. We talked about the importance of being able to work together as a team. We also discussed some of the difficulties of working as a member of a team.

In this game, students competed on teams to build towers from blocks. Teams who were patient and worked together usually had the tallest towers.

At home tonight, you can talk about some of your favorite sports teams or musical groups. Talk about how they work together to be successful. You can encourage your child to be a great team player!

Thanks for your support,

Chapter Two

Reflection

Games in this chapter concentrate on self-esteem, positive communication, understanding, and communicating feelings, anger control, and social skills for grades PK-2.

Positive Hot Potato

Grade Levels
PK - 2

Materials
• CD or Cassette Player
• Musical CD or Cassette
• Two Different Colored Balls

Time Needed
Approximately 30 minutes

Skills Covered
• Self-Esteem
• Social Skills
• Respecting Differences

Introduction

This game adds a fun twist to the game of hot potato by allowing students to say something positive about themselves, as well as something positive about other students.

Pre-Game Directions

1. Talk to the students about things they like about themselves. Ask them if they like it when people say nice things to them. Explain that we all have great qualities about us.

2. Explain to the students that we will be playing a game that will help us to think about the great things about ourselves, as well as those of others.

3. Ask the students if they have played the game of "Hot Potato" before. Show the students one of the balls and explain that this will be our hot potato. Music will play while the students sit in a circle and quickly pass the ball to one another - as if it were a hot potato. If the ball is thrown or if someone drops the ball, that person will be "out." Also, if students are talking loudly or are disrespectful to others, they are "out." When the music stops, the person holding the ball will stand up. He/she will need to say something great about him/herself. In addition, he/she will need to say something great about the person on his/her right.

4. Have a practice round and let the students practice passing the ball to one another without the music playing.

Game Directions

1. Seat the students in a circle.

2. Give one person the ball and instruct him/her to begin passing the ball when you begin playing the music.

3. Tell students they are "out" if they are caught throwing the ball, dropping the ball, talking loudly, or being disrespectful to others.

4. Stop the music after each person in the circle has had at least one turn to pass the ball. The student that is holding the ball needs to say something positive about him/herself as well as something positive about the person on his/her right.

Game #9

Grade Levels

PK - 2

Materials

- CD or Cassette Player
- Musical CD or Cassette
- Two Different Colored Balls

Time Needed

Approximately 30 minutes

Skills Covered

- Self-Esteem
- Social Skills
- Respecting Differences

Positive Hot Potato

Game Variations

- Reverse the direction in which the ball is passed.
- Add one or two more balls to the game.
- Pass the ball(s) with eyes closed.

Follow-Up

- Why do you think it is important to say nice things about other people?
- How did it feel when people said nice things about you during the game?
- Think of two people who often say nice things and compliment others. Do you like to be around these people?

Dear Parents/Guardians,

Today, your child participated in a classroom guidance game entitled, "Positive Hot Potato." The objective of this game was to teach students ways to positively communicate with each other and ways to promote positive self-esteem. We talked about how great it feels for people to say nice things to us. We discussed the importance of saying positive things to one another.

In this game, music played as students quickly passed a ball around a circle. When the music stopped, the student holding the ball had to say something positive about him/herself as well something positive about the person to his/her right.

At home tonight, you can play a quick game of "Positive Hot Potato" with your family. You can encourage family members to share positive comments about themselves and each other.

Thanks for your support,

Feelings Memory

Materials

• 4 Copies of Feelings Memory Cards (pg. 49)

• Velcro

• Large Piece of Poster Board

Time Needed

Approximately 30 minutes

Skills Covered

• Understanding & Communicating Feelings

• Social Skills

Introduction

This is a great way to help students improve concentration, memory, and to better understand the meaning of feelings.

Pre-Game Directions

1. Make 4 copies of Feelings Memory Cards and cut them out. These should also be laminated if possible.

2. Put small piece of Velcro on side of card with writing.

3. Put forty pieces of opposite side of Velcro on poster board for each of the Feelings Memory Cards.

4. Hang poster board with memory cards in front of classroom.

5. Go over the meaning of the feeling words on the Feelings Memory Cards.

6. Help students think of some times they have felt these feelings.

7. Explain to students that they will be competing on teams to match the feelings cards. Teams get one point for each match and an additional point if the player describes a time he/she felt the feeling written on the matched cards.

8. Divide the class into two teams.

Game Directions

1. Player from Team A chooses two Feelings Memory Cards and turns them over. Player shows these two cards to the class. If cards do not match, player returns cards to their places on the board. If they match, Team A gets one point. Team A gets an additional point if player describes a time he/she felt the feeling written on the matched cards.

2. Team B continues as Team A.

3. Game continues as time allows. The team with the most points wins the game.

Follow-Up

• Which of the feelings did you like talking about the most? Which of the feelings did you like talking about the least?

• Name a person with whom you feel comfortable talking about your feelings. Why is it easy to talk to this person?

• How can you tell how someone is feeling? Can you tell by what he/she is saying? Can you tell by the look on his/her face? Can you tell by the way he/she is acting?

Feelings Memory Cards

Happy   Happy

Happy   Happy

Sad   Sad

Sad   Sad

Surprised   Surprised

Surprised   Surprised

Scared   Scared

Scared   Scared

Angry   Angry

Angry   Angry

Excited   Excited

Excited   Excited

Disappointed   Disappointed

Disappointed   Disappointed

Nervous   Nervous

Nervous   Nervous

Embarrassed   Embarrassed

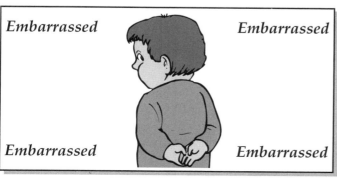

Embarrassed   Embarrassed

Thrilled   Thrilled

Thrilled   Thrilled

Dear Parents/Guardians,

Today, your child participated in a classroom guidance game entitled, "Feelings Memory." The objective of this game was to help students understand their own feelings, as well as the feelings of others. Ten different feeling words were discussed. Students were encouraged to share times they felt these feelings.

In this game, students competed on teams to match pairs of feelings. Players described times they felt these emotions for additional points.

At home tonight, you can help your children expand their feelings vocabulary. You can encourage your child to share new feelings words with you. You can even play a game with your family where you list as many feeling words as possible.

Thanks for your support,

Don't Let Your Snowman Have a Meltdown!

Game #11

Grade Levels

PK - 2

Materials

- 2 Copies of Snowman (pg.53)
- 2 Copies of Snowman Accessories (pg.54)
- 1 Copy of the Snowman Question Cards (pp.55-56)
- Velcro or Paper Clips
- Tape

Time Needed

Approximately 30 minutes

Skills Covered

- Anger Control
- Appropriate Ways to Deal With Anger

Introduction

This is a fun way to teach students the importance of dealing with anger in appropriate ways. In this game, hot, inappropriate actions cause snowmen to melt. Appropriate ways to deal with anger keep the snowmen from melting. Teams compete against each other to keep their snowmen from melting.

Pre-Game Directions

1. Make two copies of the Snowman.

2. Make two copies of the Snowman Accessories.

3. Copy and cut out the Snowman Question Cards. If possible, laminate the Snowman Question Cards.

4. Use Velcro or paper clips to attach the Snowman Accessories to the two Snowmen.

5. Tape the two Snowmen on the board in front of the classroom.

6. When stacking the cards, make sure that the first ten are those that describe inappropriate actions.

7. Explain to the class that we will be learning appropriate ways to deal with anger. Ask the students if it is okay to be angry. Explain that it is okay to be angry, but we need to make sure our actions are appropriate.

8. Ask the students about some inappropriate ways to deal with anger. For example:
   - "Is it okay to hit people?"
   - "Is it okay to yell at your mom?"
   - "Is it okay to tear up your math work?"
   - Talk about how these actions can hurt people.

9. Ask the students about some appropriate ways to deal with anger. For example:
   - "Is it okay to draw when you are angry?"
   - "Is it okay to take a rest when you are angry?"
   - "Is it okay to ask for time alone when you are angry?"
   - Talk about how these actions can help people calm down so that they will not hurt anyone.

10. Explain to the class that you will be playing a game where the students will choose cards that describe either inappropriate or appropriate ways to deal with anger. Each team will have a snowman. Inappropriate actions will cause the snowmen to melt by removing accessories. Appropriate actions will keep the snowmen from melting by adding accessories.

Game #11

Grade Levels
PK - 2

Materials
- 2 Copies of Snowman (pg.53)
- 2 Copies of Snowman Accessories (pg.54)
- 1 Copy of the Snowman Question Cards (pp.55-56)
- Velcro or Paper Clips
- Tape

Time Needed
Approximately 30 minutes

Skills Covered
- Anger Control
- Appropriate Ways to Deal With Anger

Don't Let Your Snowman Have a Meltdown!

Game Directions

1. Divide class into two teams.

2. Player from Team A picks a Snowman Question Card.

3. Player determines if action described on card is an appropriate or inappropriate way to deal with anger. If it is appropriate, player adds a Snowman Accessory. If the action is inappropriate, player removes an accessory from his team's snowman.

4. Player from Team B continues in same manner.

5. Game continues as time allows or one of the snowmen loses all of his accessories.

Follow-Up

- What are some situations in which it is hard to stay calm and not lose your temper? How do you stay calm during these times?
- Describe a time that you did a great job of staying calm when someone made you angry.
- What are some new ideas that you learned today that will help you deal with your anger in appropriate ways?

Snowman Accessories

Snowman Question Cards

Finn threw a ball at Natalie because he was mad at her.

Jessie broke a glass because he was mad at his mom.

Nicole did not understand her math so she broke her pencil.

Winona was frustrated with reading so she threw her book on the floor.

Terry was mad because she did not win the race so he hits Tommy.

James tripped Jessica because he was in a bad mood.

Grace pushed Mary because Mary called Grace a name.

Heather hit Beth because Beth talked about Heather's mom.

Miguel smacked Winston because Winston rolled his eyes at Miguel.

Annette shoved Devon because Devon said he was going to take her lunch.

Justin hit his pillow in his room because he was in a bad mood.

Felicia ran around and played at home because she had a bad day at school.

Amanda talked to her teacher about how she feels when Shawn will not sit by her at lunch.

Breanna shook her fist at Rosita and threatened to punch her because she was mad.

Kim talked to a friend about how she feels when her brother takes her toys from her.

Snowman Question Cards

Julie talked to her teacher about how she feels when she has trouble with her math.

Sydney colored and drew pictures because she was frustrated and needed to take a break.

Gabriel played basketball with his brother because his friends hurt his feelings.

Corina threw rocks at her mom's car because her mom made her mad.

Shelley watched a movie with her mom because her friends did not want to play with her.

Kelly jumped on her trampoline to help get out her angry feelings about reading.

Marissa helped her dad cook dinner because her brother was picking on her.

Tempest rested in her room after her friends were mean to her.

Troy played outside because his little brothers kept messing with all of his toys.

Katrina wrote in her diary because she was mad at her parents.

Sunita pushed her brother because she was mad at her parents.

Katie played a game with her dad because her friend said that nobody likes her.

Krissy talked to her grandma about how she feels when people pick on her on the bus.

Suzy yelled at her friend and called her names because she was mad at her.

Victoria talked to her counselor about how she feels when Ronnie calls her names.

Dear Parents/Guardians,

Today, your child participated in a classroom guidance game entitled, "Don't Let Your Snowman Have a Meltdown." The objective of this game was to teach students positive ways to deal with their anger. We talked about how it is okay to be angry, but it is not okay to act inappropriately.

In this game, students competed against each other on two teams. Each team was given a fully dressed paper snowman. Players picked cards describing ways to deal with anger. Inappropriate ways to deal with anger caused the snowmen to lose some of their accessories, while appropriate ways to deal with anger added accessories to the snowmen.

At home tonight, you can encourage your child to talk about his/her best ways to deal with anger. For example, maybe your child loves to run around outside. Therefore, spending some time outside would be a great way for him/her to deal with anger.

Thanks for your support,

Game #12

Copyright YouthLight, Inc.

Grade Levels

PK - 2

Materials

- Three Hula Hoops
- One Small Beanbag
- Copy of the Beanbag Toss Cards (pp.59-60)

Time Needed

Approximately 30 minutes

Skills Covered

- Anger Control
- Appropriate Ways to Deal With Anger

Anger Control Beanbag Toss

Introduction

This game is a great way for students to demonstrate their knowledge of appropriate ways to control their anger while engaging in a game of beanbag toss!

Pre-Game Directions

1. Copy and cut out Beanbag Toss Cards.

2. Mark a place for the students to stand when tossing the beanbag.

3. Place the first hula hoop about two feet away from the marker where the students will stand. Mark this hula hoop #1.

4. Place the second hula hoop about four feet away from the marker where the students will stand. Mark this hula hoop #2.

5. Place the third hula hoop about six feet away from the marker where the students will stand. Mark this hula hoop #3.

6. Ask the class about appropriate ways to deal with anger. Ask them to give examples of times they have dealt appropriately with anger.

7. Help the class think of many ways to deal with anger such as: talking to your parent/guardian, asking someone for help, taking a break, playing outside, playing a game, or talking to one of your friends.

Game Directions

1. Divide the class into two teams.

2. Each student will have a turn to pick a Beanbag Toss Card. The Beanbag Toss Cards depict scenarios where someone is angry. In order to get one point, the student needs to think of an appropriate way to deal with the anger.

3. The student has the opportunity to earn additional points by tossing the beanbag into one of the hula hoops. Hula Hoop #1 earns one additional point. Hula Hoop #2 earns two additional points. Hula Hoop #3 earns three additional points.

4. Teams compete against each other for points. The team with the most points wins the game!

Game Variation

- Game can be played as described above, but students must describe an actual or fictional time that they felt anger and an appropriate way that they handled the anger.

Beanbag Toss Cards

Chelsea is frustrated because she cannot understand her math homework.

Noah is upset because his brother is not sharing the computer.

Stella is mad because someone keeps poking her in the head on the bus.

Lin is upset because Tyler keeps copying her classwork.

Taylor is mad because no one will play with her at recess.

Carlos is in a bad mood because he is worried about the note his teacher sent home to his parents.

Yvonne is mad because she does not like doing homework.

Mya is mad because her mom punished her for disobeying.

Elijah is embarrassed because his friends made fun of his shoes.

Rita is mad because Charlotte would not sit beside her on the bus.

Delisha is mad because Avery said she would not invite her to her birthday party.

Maria is in a bad mood because she is worried about her science test.

Destiny is mad because her mom makes her wear her glasses to school.

Terrence is upset because he thinks his teacher does not like him.

Anthony is mad because his friends made fun of him.

Beanbag Toss Cards

Jamison is mad because no one would pick him for the kickball team.

Blair is embarrassed because he has to wear his brother's old coat.

Isaac is embarrassed because he is shorter than everyone in his class.

Derek is upset because his brother made fun of the way he runs.

Erick is frustrated because he has trouble hitting a baseball.

Katelyn is upset because her family cannot afford to buy her new shoes.

Clarence is frustrated because he cannot keep up with his class when they read out loud.

Darcy is mad because her dad yelled at her for not cleaning up her room.

Jessica is frustrated because she did her homework and now she can't find it.

Abraham is mad because he ripped his new pants.

Candy is mad because her mom made her get a haircut that she does not like.

Lexie is mad because her sister got more new clothes than she did.

Tripp is mad because he lost his snack money and now he cannot get a snack after lunch.

Rosia is frustrated because she tries very hard, but she has trouble learning at school.

Nicholas is upset because Sidney did not talk to him at school.

Dear Parents/Guardians,

Today, your child participated in a classroom guidance game entitled, "Anger Control Beanbag Toss." The objective of this game was to encourage student to control their anger. We discussed many different ways to release anger appropriately such as going outside, reading a book, taking a rest, talking to someone, and playing a game.

In this game, students competed on two teams. Players picked cards that described situations that often cause anger. In order to receive a point, players had to explain an appropriate way they would deal with their anger in this situation. Teams received additional points if players successfully tossed beanbags inside hula hoops.

At home tonight, you can encourage your child to talk about different ways that he/she learned to control anger in our game today. You can encourage your child to practice using one of these techniques the next time he/she is angry.

Thanks for your support,

Levels

'K - 2

rials

- ... Paper Lunch Bags
- Copy of Feeling Faces (pg.63)
- Copy of Emotional Match Cards (pp.64-65)
- Tape or Glue

Time Needed

Approximately 30 minutes

Skills Covered

- Social Skills
- Understanding and Communicating Feelings

Emotional Match

Introduction

This game is really fun for younger students. Even students who have difficulty with reading will have a wonderful time matching the scenarios with the feeling faces.

Pre-Game Directions

1. Copy and cut out Emotional Match Cards and Eight Feeling Faces.

2. Tape or glue each of the Eight Feeling Faces to the front of one of the paper bags.

3. Show the class each of the faces on the paper bags.

4. Talk about the meaning of each of the feeling faces.

5. Help the students think of times they have felt the emotions on the feeling faces.

6. Place the paper bags in front of the class where the students can see the Feeling Faces.

7. Explain to the class that everyone will be participating in a game where the students will choose one of the Feelings Match Cards and will get to put the card in the bag with the Feeling Face that matches the scenario.

8. Have a practice round for the class. Give the class a scenario for each emotion and ask them to guess which Feeling Face matches this scenario.
   - Katrina got a present from her aunt in the mail. – **surprised**
   - Sarah fell down and people laughed at her. – **embarrassed**
   - Johnny thinks monsters are in his closet. – **scared**
   - Tico has a lot of trouble reading. – **frustrated**
   - Marissa's friend hurt her feelings. – **sad**
   - Gordon wants to hit his brother. – **angry**
   - Nina is watching a movie with her mother. – **happy**
   - Carlos is having a birthday party tomorrow. – **excited**

Game Directions

1. Each student picks an Emotional Match Card and places it in the bag with the Feeling Face that matches the scenario on the card.

2. Game continues until all students have had a turn. Some scenarios may be able to be placed in more than one bag. For example:
   - Carlos is having a birthday party tomorrow. – **excited or happy**

Follow-Up

- Give each student one of the emotions in the game. Instruct the students to draw a picture that represents that emotion.

Surprised

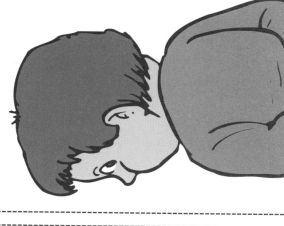

Embarrassed

Scared

Frustrated

Sad

Angry

Happy

Excited

Emotional Match Cards

| Happy | Angry | Sad | Scared | Surprised | Excited | Embarrassed | Frustrated |

Anna shoved her brother.

David feels nervous around his parents' friends because he has not met them before.

Marcus thinks there is a monster under his bed.

Rose does not like to go outside at night.

Sergio is having a great time painting in art class.

Miranda is worried about going to a new babysitter.

Ariel yelled at her sister because she messed up her room.

Kelsey is crying.

Dana got a good note sent home from her teacher.

Jermelle made a new friend.

Ishmael got a new puppy.

Adam's grandmother is in the hospital and is very sick.

Emily has to go to a new school and meet new friends.

Jose's teacher sent a note home to his parents because he was not listening.

Travis does not want to go to his gymnastics class.

Emotional Match Cards

Happy Angry Sad Scared Surprised Excited Embarrassed Frustrated *Magda is playing basketball with her friends.*	**Happy Angry Sad Scared Surprised Excited Embarrassed Frustrated** *Larry's friends said that he cannot play with them during recess.*	**Happy Angry Sad Scared Surprised Excited Embarrassed Frustrated** *Frances did not get a chance to kick the ball during the soccer game.*
Happy Angry Sad Scared Surprised Excited Embarrassed Frustrated *Penny's mom said that she cannot sleep over at a friend's house.*	**Happy Angry Sad Scared Surprised Excited Embarrassed Frustrated** *Holly got a new bike.*	**Happy Angry Sad Scared Surprised Excited Embarrassed Frustrated** *Margo learned how to dive off the diving board.*
Happy Angry Sad Scared Surprised Excited Embarrassed Frustrated *Jared won the race.*	**Happy Angry Sad Scared Surprised Excited Embarrassed Frustrated** *Terrence doesn't think his drawings ever look right.*	**Happy Angry Sad Scared Surprised Excited Embarrassed Frustrated** *Cole yelled at his friends because they made fun of him.*
Happy Angry Sad Scared Surprised Excited Embarrassed Frustrated *Trudy did not get invited to a birthday party.*	**Happy Angry Sad Scared Surprised Excited Embarrassed Frustrated** *Jennifer is playing outside with her friends.*	**Happy Angry Sad Scared Surprised Excited Embarrassed Frustrated** *Owen is going to the circus tomorrow.*
Happy Angry Sad Scared Surprised Excited Embarrassed Frustrated *Quentin cannot find his favorite toy.*	**Happy Angry Sad Scared Surprised Excited Embarrassed Frustrated** *Perry's neighbor has big dogs that bark and growl at him.*	**Happy Angry Sad Scared Surprised Excited Embarrassed Frustrated** *Devon is playing a game with his brother.*

Dear Parents/Guardians,

Today, your child participated in a classroom guidance game entitled, "Emotional Match." The objective of this game was to teach students ways to understand their own emotions, as well as those of others. In our lesson, we discussed eight different emotions: surprised, embarrassed, happy, sad, angry, frustrated, scared, and excited. Students shared times they have felt these emotions.

In this game, students matched scenarios with a feeling face that depicted each emotion. Each student picked a scenario card and decided which emotion matched the situation described on that card.

At home tonight, you can review the eight emotions from our game. Your family members can take turns sharing times they have felt these emotions!

Thanks for your support,

Draw Your Feelings!

Introduction

This game is really fun for students to get a chance to draw and expand upon their vocabulary of feelings.

Pre-Game Directions

1. Copy and cut out the Draw Your Feelings Cards.

2. Go over the Draw Your Feelings Cards with the class.

3. Help students think of examples for each of these words: **bashful, nervous, excited, happy, sad, depressed, angry, bored, peaceful, loving, frustrated, and proud.**

4. Explain to the class that we will be playing a game with the feelings words. The class will be divided into two teams.

5. Each student will choose a card and then will have a turn to try to draw a picture that depicts and describes this card. The team will have two minutes to guess the feeling drawn by the student.

6. The team gets one point for guessing the feeling and an additional point if the student describes a time that he/she felt this feeling.

Game Directions

1. Player from Team A picks card and has one minute to draw a picture that depicts this feeling while Team A guesses.

2. Team A gets one point if they guess the feeling in the allotted two minutes. Team A can get an additional point if the player can describe a time he/she felt this feeling.

3. Team B proceeds as Team A.

4. Continue game as time allows.

5. The team with the most points wins the game.

Follow-Up

- Do you think it is important to be able to explain to others how you are feeling? Why or why not?
- Do you think it is important to be able to tell how others are feeling? Why or why not?
- What kinds of problems do you think can be prevented if people are willing to talk about how they feel?

Grade Levels

PK - 2

Materials

- Markers or Crayons
- Whiteboard or Large Pieces of Paper
- Copy of Draw Your Feelings Cards (pg.68)

Time Needed

Approximately 30 minutes

Skills Covered

- Social Skills
- Understanding and Communicating Feelings

Draw Your Feelings Cards

Bashful

Nervous

Excited

Happy

Sad

Depressed

Angry

Bored

Peaceful

Loving

Proud

Frustrated

Dear Parents/Guardians,

Today, your child participated in a classroom guidance game entitled, "Draw Your Feelings." The objective of this game was to help students increase their vocabularies of emotional words. We discussed the meaning of the following words: bashful, nervous, excited, happy, sad, depressed, angry, bored, peaceful, loving, frustrated, and proud. Children often have difficulty describing the way they feel and may limit themselves to using only a few words such as sad and mad.

In this game, students were divided into two teams. Players picked cards with emotion words. Players had to draw situations depicting the emotions and their teams had to guess the appropriate emotion words.

At home tonight, you can talk to your child about the importance of being able to talk to someone about how they feel. You can encourage your child to continue to talk to you about his/her feelings.

Thanks for your support,

Game #15

Grade Levels

PK - 2

Materials

• Copy of Crayon Handout for Each Student (pg.72)

• Tape

• Crayons, Markers, and Colored Pencils

• Box of Crayons

• Box of Crayons Containing Crayons of Only One Color

• Poster Board / Butcher Paper

Time Needed

Approximately 30 minutes

Skills Covered

• Social Skills

• Self-Esteem

• Respecting Differences

The Crayon Game

Introduction

This game promotes self-esteem and gives students a chance to be proud of their individual and unique characteristics.

Pre-Game Directions

1. Show the students the box of many colored crayons. Talk about the different colors in the box. Talk about how great it is to be able to use the many colors to draw great pictures.

2. Show the students the box of same-colored crayons. Talk about how boring this box of crayons is. Talk about how difficult it would be to draw a picture of someone playing outside if only one color could be used.

3. Talk to the class about how we are all different – like the box of many-colored crayons. Explain to them that our differences are what makes each of us special and unique.

4. Explain to the class that sometimes people do not respect us and may tease us about our special characteristics. When people tease us, it may hurt our feelings and may make us embarrassed or self-conscious about our differences.

5. Talk about how boring our class would be if we were all exactly the same – if we all looked the same, played the same sports, colored the same pictures, etc. Therefore, we should embrace our differences and be very proud of what we contribute to our class and our world.

6. Explain to the class that everyone will get the opportunity to color one of the paper crayons and complete one of the following sentences on the back of the crayon:

    I love my _____ because _____.
    Or for Pre-K and Kindergarten students:
    I love my _____.

7. Give the students an example of something they can write on their crayon. For example, I always say "I love my big feet because they make me run fast."

The Crayon Game

Game Directions

1. Give each child a copy of a paper crayon. Instruct each child to color the crayon his/her favorite color.

2. Instruct each child to write down and complete the sentence, "I like my _____ because _____" on the back of the paper crayon.

3. Collect the completed paper crayons.

4. Read the back of each crayon, one at a time. Give the class three guesses to figure out which student completed each crayon.

5. After the class guesses, tape each paper crayon to the poster board. When complete, the poster board should resemble a box of multi-colored crayons.

Follow-Up

• Supply construction paper, scissors, and crayons to create different pieces of fruit for a fruit basket, different instruments for a band, or different pieces of candy for a candy box. Have students decorate and write down their talents on their pieces of paper.

Grade Levels

PK - 2

Materials

• Copy of Crayon Handout for Each Student (pg.72)

• Tape

• Crayons, Markers, and Colored Pencils

• Box of Crayons

• Box of Crayons Containing Crayons of Only One Color

• Poster Board / Butcher Paper

Time Needed

Approximately 30 minutes

Skills Covered

• Social Skills

• Self-Esteem

• Respecting Differences

I Am Special

Dear Parents/Guardians,

Today, your child participated in a classroom guidance game entitled, "The Crayon Game." The objective of this game was to encourage students to be proud of their individual, unique characteristics. We talked about how boring it would be if all crayons were the same color. We discussed the importance of having lots of colored crayons and the importance of having lots of different people around us!

In this game, students colored paper crayons and wrote down the thing they love the most about themselves. Students guessed which student made each crayon. All crayons were glued on a poster board to create a classroom set of individual crayons and personalities.

At home tonight, encourage your child to talk about things that he/she loves about him/herself. Encourage your child to be proud of these individual traits!

Thanks for your support,

Communication Charades

els
- 2

als
de
5)

Time Needed

Approximately 30 minutes

Skills Covered

• Social Skills

• Understanding and Communicating Feelings

Introduction

This game is really fun for all students. It is easy for everyone to play because it only requires nonverbal skills.

Pre-Game Directions

1. Make two copies of the Charade Cards.

2. Cut out and stack the Charade Cards.

3. Talk to the students about how our faces and our bodies can talk to others – just like actual words. For example, cross your arms and give an angry look. Ask the students to guess how you feel. When they guess angry, ask them to explain how they could tell that you were angry. Let them describe the different characteristics that showed them your anger.

4. Go over the feeling words on the cards. Act out each one and let the class guess which emotion you are portraying.

5. Explain to the class that they will be participating in a game where they will have the opportunity to silently act out the feeling words. The class will be divided into two teams. Each team will have thirty seconds to guess the feeling. If they correctly guess the feeling within thirty seconds, their team will get a point. Each feeling word is used two times on the Charade Cards.

6. Divide class into two teams.

Game Directions

1. Player from Team A picks a Charade Card. Player has thirty seconds to act out the feeling while team tries to guess the feeling. If the team guesses correctly within thirty seconds, they earn one point.

2. Player from Team B continues as Team A.

3. Game continues as time allows. Team with most points wins.

Follow-Up

• Have you ever talked to someone who said that she was happy, but her facial expression looked sad or mad? Which did you believe – the expression on her face (sad or mad) or the words she said (happy)? Explain why.

• Which do you think is more important – the way that we look and act or the words that we use in describing our feelings?

• Is it difficult for you to hide your feelings if you are really excited, really happy, really sad, or really mad? Please explain.

Charade Cards

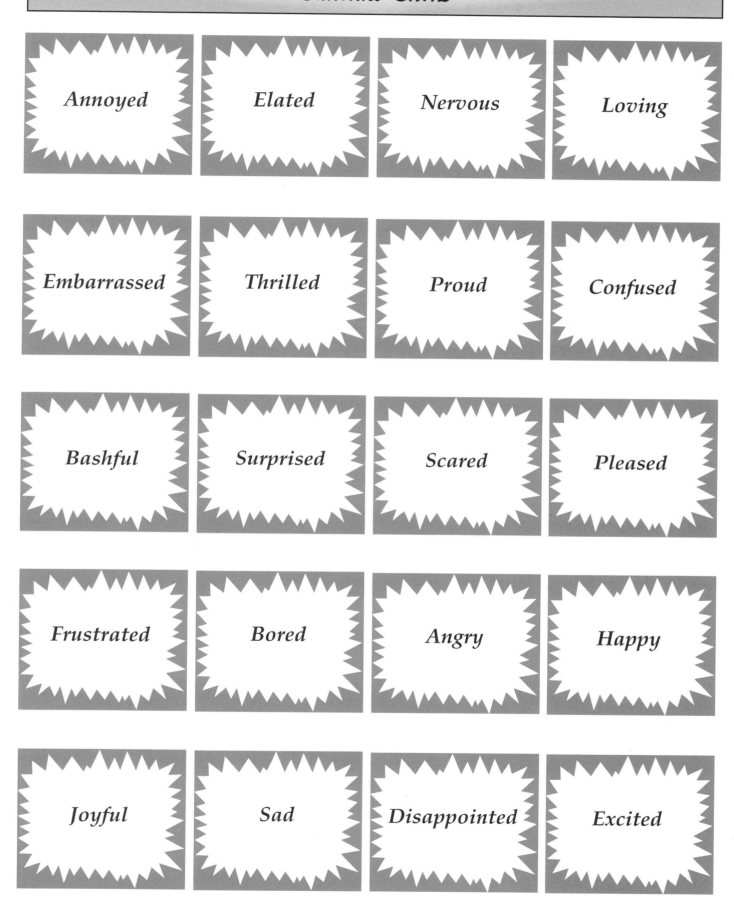

Annoyed	Elated	Nervous	Loving
Embarrassed	Thrilled	Proud	Confused
Bashful	Surprised	Scared	Pleased
Frustrated	Bored	Angry	Happy
Joyful	Sad	Disappointed	Excited

Dear Parents/Guardians,

Today, your child participated in a classroom guidance game entitled, "Communication Charades." The objective of this game was to teach students ways to communicate their feelings with one another. We talked about how our actions show others how we are feeling even more than our words show them.

In this game, students competed against each other on two teams. Players picked cards describing emotions. Players then had to silently act out the emotions for their teams while the teams had to guess the correct emotion.

At home tonight, you could play a simple game of Communication Charades. Family members could use their facial expressions to show different emotions. Everyone can guess what emotion is being depicted.

Thanks for your support,

Chapter Three

Responsibility

Games in this chapter concentrate on goal setting, study skills, and career information for grades PK-2.

Game #17

Grade Levels
PK - 2

Materials
• Copy of Do the Right Thing Tic-Tac-Toe Cards (pp.80-81)

Time Needed
Approximately 30 minutes

Skills Covered
• Responsible Behaviors
• Making the Right Decisions

Do the Right Thing Tic-Tac-Toe

Introduction
Students have a great time playing the game of tic-tac-toe while practicing ways to behave responsibly.

Pre-Game Directions

1. Copy and cut out the Do the Right Thing Tic-Tac-Toe Cards.

2. Draw a tic-tac-toe board on the chalkboard or whiteboard.

3. Explain to the class that they will be participating in an exciting game of tic-tac-toe.

4. Explain that in this game of tic-tac-toe, students will be given questions from the Do the Right Thing Tic-Tac-Toe Cards. These questions focus on responsible actions towards themselves, others, and the world around them.

5. Review responsible behaviors with the students. Ask the students to explain what the word "responsible" means to them. Explain that when people behave responsibly they consider the feelings of themselves, the feelings of others, and the world around them. Responsible people do what they say they will do, when they are supposed to do it.

6. Tell the students that they will be on two different teams – the X's and the O's. Teams will get the opportunity to place an X or an O on the tic-tac-toe board after correctly answering a Do the Right Thing Tic-Tac-Toe Card.

Game Directions

1. Begin game by giving each team 5 points. These points can be taken away for any unsportsmanlike behaviors. Hopefully this will ensure that students will be able to place an X or an O anywhere on the Tic-Tac-Toe board – without having other students complain about the students' choices.

2. Player from X team picks card from Do the Right Thing Tic-Tac-Toe Cards and answers the question.

3. If answered correctly, team X can place an X on the Tic-Tac-Toe Board.

4. Player from O team continues as X team – but places an O on the Tic-Tac-Toe Board if the question is correctly answered.

Do the Right Thing
Tic-Tac-Toe

Grade Levels
PK - 2
Materials
• Copy of Do the Right Thing Tic-Tac-Toe Cards (pp.80-81)
Time Needed
Approximately 30 minutes
Skills Covered
• Responsible Behaviors
• Making the Right Decisions

Game Directions continued...

5. Game continues until three X's or three O's are in a row – or until the board is full. If a team gets three X's or three O's in a row – that team will get one point. If there is no winner, both teams get a point.

6. Continue playing game, but allow player from team O to begin this game. Winner gets one point – or in case of no winner, both teams get a point.

7. Play as many games as time allows. Winner has most points.

Game Variation

• In order to put an X or an O on the tic-tac-toe board, students must explain a time that they or someone they know did the right thing in a difficult situation.

Do The Right Thing Tic-Tac-Toe Cards

Your mom says you have to finish your math homework before you go outside. You really want to go outside, but you have a lot of math to do. You are considering writing down anything just to finish. What should you do?

Your dad told you to clean up your room before you watch television. It's time for your favorite show and your room is almost done. What should you do?

You told your best friend you would sit beside her in lunch today. However, when lunch arrives, you want to sit beside someone else. What should you do?

You told your sister you would help her with her art project after school. However, after school your friend asked you to come over and play. What should you do?

You signed up for soccer. However, on the third day of practice, you are tired and just want to stay home and watch television. What should you do?

You told your friend you would come over to play after school. However, another friend asked you to come over and you would rather go over to his house. What should you do?

You did your math homework and your science homework. You really don't like reading too much and you don't want to do your reading homework. What should you do?

Your teacher told you to read a story and then draw a picture. The story is really hard to read and you want to start drawing the picture because that seems like more fun. What should you do?

Your teacher said that you need to eat part of your lunch before you can eat your ice cream. You saw someone else eating her ice cream before she ate her lunch. What should you do?

You promised your mom you would clean the kitchen after you finished playing outside. However, you are really tired after you finish playing. What should you do?

You told one of your friends that you would go to her birthday party on Saturday. After you tell her this, someone else invites you to another birthday party that you would rather attend. What should you do?

Your teacher told you to do your math work first and then your reading. You really don't like math too much, and you want to do the reading work first. What should you do?

You have baseball practice after school. When you get home, you are tired and don't want to do your homework. What should you do?

You told your stepmom that you would watch your little brother while she takes a shower. He is really getting on your nerves and you would rather play with your game. What should you do?

Your papa said that he needs someone to help him clean out the cars this afternoon. You told him that you would help. However, your neighbor asked you to come over to play football this afternoon. What should you do?

Do The Right Thing Tic-Tac-Toe Cards

Your teacher has asked all students to put everything away in its proper place before leaving each day. You are really in a hurry to get to the bus and you just want to throw everything in your desk. What should you do?

Your teacher has asked that everyone wash his/her hands before eating lunch. You are starving and really want to get to lunch quickly. You don't think she will notice if you don't wash your hands. What do you think?

Your teacher has asked that you hang up your coat and backpack each day. You tried to hang yours up but it fell off the hook. You are already tired and in a hurry to get to your desk and start your morning work. What should you do?

Your friend asked you to help him practice throwing the football and you agreed to help him. Another friend has now asked you to come over and play in a football game. What should you do?

You told your sister she could borrow your new scarf and wear it to school. Unfortunately, now you really want to wear it. What should you do?

You told your grandmother that you would play cards with your family for Family Night. You just realized that your favorite movie is coming on television at the same time and you really want to watch it. What should you do?

Your parents paid for you to join a softball team. They asked that you use your allowance to help pay for the new glove you need. When you get your allowance, you realize that you really want to buy a new CD instead. What should you do?

You told your friend that you would play with her at recess. Another one of your friends said that if you play with anyone else except for her, she will not speak to you anymore. What should you do?

Your mom said that you can bring two friends with you to the movies. You invited two friends, but then realized that there is someone else you would rather have go to the movies with you. What should you do?

Your mom gave you $1.00 and said that you can buy one snack. She asked you to bring her the change. You decide that you really want two snacks. What should you do?

You borrowed a book from the library. You have to bring it back to school on Tuesday. On Monday night, you are too tired to figure out where you put the book and you just want to go to bed. What should you do?

You wake up really tired and you just don't feel like going to school. You'd rather stay at home and watch television. What should you do?

You borrowed a game from one of your friends. They asked you to bring it back the next day. The next day, you decide that you would like to keep it longer because it is a really cool game. What should you do?

You love to go to P.E. However, you don't love the library. You want to go to the clinic to rest during library time, but you want to leave in time for P.E. What should you do?

You miss your mom at school. You think that if you act sick you might get to go home and see her. What should you do?

Dear Parents/Guardians,

Today, your child participated in a classroom guidance game entitled, "Do the Right Thing Tic-Tac-Toe." The objective of this game was to teach students the importance of being responsible and doing the right thing – even when it is difficult to do so. We talked about how we need to act responsibly towards ourselves, others, and the world around us.

In this game, students were divided into two teams – the X's and the O's. In order to place an X or an O on our tic-tac-toe board, students had to answer questions about ways to act responsibly.

At home tonight, you can praise your child for a time when he/she did the right thing and acted responsibly. For example, maybe your child does not love reading, but still did his reading homework.

Thanks for your support,

Responsible Basketball

Game #18

Grade Levels
PK - 2

Materials
- Small Basketball Hoop or Bucket / Basket
- Small Ball
- Copy of Responsible Basketball Cards (pp.84-85)

Time Needed
Approximately 30 minutes

Skills Covered
- Goal Setting
- Decision-Making Skills
- Study Skills

Introduction
A fabulous game for all to play – lots of opportunities to practice responsible actions as well as the chance to shoot a few hoops!

Pre-Game Directions
1. Place basketball hoop/bucket/basket in front of room.

2. Copy and cut out Responsible Basketball Cards.

3. Explain to class that you will be playing a special game of basketball where teams can earn points by correctly answering questions about responsible behaviors.

4. If a player answers a question correctly, the team will receive two points and the player will then have the opportunity to shoot the ball into the "basket" for two extra points.

5. Review the importance of responsible behaviors. Ask students about the difficulties of sometimes doing the right thing, even when we would rather do something else. Explain that doing the right thing often involves being brave and not caring what others think of us. For example, if there is someone in your class that everyone is teasing, you should be brave and do the right thing by being nice to that person.

Game Directions
1. Divide class into two teams.

2. Player from Team A draws a Responsible Basketball Card. Player must decide how he/she would act in this situation. Team A gets two points for appropriate answers.

3. Player A then gets an opportunity to receive two additional points by shooting the "basketball" into the "basket."

4. Team B proceeds as Team A.

5. Game proceeds as time allows. The team with most points wins the game.

Follow-Up
- What are some situations where you were brave and did the right thing, even when others were not doing so?
- Do you think it is important to do the things that we promise or commit that we will do? Do you think it is important that people believe in us? Why/why not?
- What are some times of the day when it is probably important to check and make sure that you have everything that you need?

Responsible Basketball Cards

Jade said that if you sit beside Isabel during lunch, Jade will not be your friend anymore. What should you do?

Cuba is teasing Peter about his pants and everyone in the class is laughing. Peter looks like he is going to cry. What should you do?

Antonio does not understand some of the words his teacher has written on the board. What should she do?

Dinah has not finished her homework, but she really wants to watch television. What should she do?

Chelsea is supposed to practice her math. Should she practice it at home before dinner, the next morning before she wakes up, or on the bus?

Jolene is supposed to visit her grandmother on Sunday. However, Jolene wants to go play soccer with her friends instead of going to see her grandmother. What should she do?

Tina is doing her homework and is having a lot of trouble doing her math. What should she do?

Siobhan is part of a soccer team. She is supposed to play in a soccer game on Saturday. On Saturday, she wakes up and decides that she wants to go swimming instead. What should she do?

Latisha is getting ready to do her homework. What are some things she should have in order to make sure she does a good job with her homework?

Miranda is getting ready for the school day to end. She is packing her backpack. What should she remember to take home with her?

Vincent is getting ready to do his homework. He really wants to watch some television while he is doing his homework. Where should Vincent do his homework?

Julianna told her mom that if she let her stay up and watch a movie, she would wake up early and clean her room. The next morning, after staying up late, Julianna wakes up and does not want to clean her room because she is too tired. What should she do?

Yolanda cannot find her notebook where she wrote down what she is supposed to do for homework and she cannot remember what she is supposed to do? What should she do?

Peyton is telling everyone not to let Derek play football. Derek asks you if he can play. What should you do?

Tristan is new at school and has not made any friends. What should you do?

Responsible Basketball Cards

Manuel is supposed to be watching his little brother while his mom cleans out the car. Manuel really wants to watch a movie. What should he do?

Cleo is packing her backpack for school tomorrow. The only thing she has packed so far is her favorite toy. What else should she put in her backpack?

Dorie is making fun of Bobbie Jo. She is telling everyone that Bobbie Jo stinks and that no one should sit beside her. What should you do?

Kareem is supposed to bring 5 extra pencils and a piece of poster board to school tomorrow. Where should he put these things before he goes to bed?

For homework, Cornelius is supposed to read his book to an adult at home. When should he start reading the book – right after school, late at night, or the next morning?

Tiara thinks that she can remember what she has to do for homework, so she does not want to write it down. Why should she write it down anyway?

Cynthia promised her dad she would help him rake leaves after school. When Cynthia gets home from school, she wants to play instead. What should she do?

Mary cannot read the directions on her math paper. What should she do?

Lucy is supposed to sing in the school musical. On the night of the musical, Lucy wants to go play at her cousin's house instead of singing in the musical. What should she do?

Trisha is in a really big hurry and does not want to stop and read all the directions on her paper. Why should she stop and read all the directions before beginning the work?

Candy is telling everyone that Amanda is a baby and wets the bed. Everyone is laughing at Amanda. What should you do?

Latrice is sitting by herself on the bus and she looks very sad. What should you do?

Kelly is supposed to be quietly reading in the library. She really wants to finish the crossword puzzle she started earlier in the day. What should she do?

Adrianna cannot remember what her teacher told the class to do. What should she do?

Juanita rushed through her work and it is very messy. What should she do?

Dear Parents/Guardians,

Today, your child participated in a classroom guidance game entitled, "Responsible Basketball." The objective of this game was to teach students the importance of behaving responsibly towards others. We talked about how it is often difficult to behave responsibly towards others because we worry about what others think of us. For example, if everyone is laughing at someone, it is very difficult to be the one that reaches out to that person.

In this game, students were divided into two teams. They picked scenario cards and had to decide if the situations described responsible actions towards others or irresponsible actions towards others. If answered correctly, teams received two points. Teams had the opportunity to gain an additional two points by shooting a small ball into our basket – the trashcan!

At home tonight, please encourage your child to continue to be brave and act responsibly towards others.

Thanks for your support,

Yellow Brick Road

Introduction

This game gets all students involved in reaching the magical "Land of Oz" by way of good decisions. Good decisions add bricks to the yellow brick road, while poor decisions take bricks away.

Pre-Game Directions

1. At the top of the classroom blackboard, place the four "Land of Oz" cards.

2. At the bottom of the classroom blackboard, place the pictures of Dorothy, Tinman, Scarecrow, and Lion.

3. Give a brief overview of the story of "The Wizard of Oz" by L. Frank Baum:

   In the story, "The Wizard of Oz," a girl named Dorothy, a Tinman, a Scarecrow, and a Lion all have something they want to achieve. They set a goal to reach the "Land of Oz," where they hope to see a wizard who will grant their wishes. Dorothy wants to go home, the Tinman wants a heart, the Scarecrow wants a brain, and the Lion wants to be brave. Dorothy, the Tinman, the Scarecrow, and the Lion are all determined to reach their goal of getting to the "Land of Oz." In order to get there, they follow a yellow brick road. On the yellow brick road, they run into many problems, but they do not give up. They keep going and they reach the "Land of Oz."

4. Talk about the following words and phrases with the class: **determination, goal setting, working together, and achievement.**

5. Ask the class about some goals that they may have and some ways they can reach these goals. For example, if someone wants to be a great soccer player, he/she should run, practice kicking the ball, and play soccer with friends. Explain that someone cannot just wake up one day and want to be a great soccer player. People have to work on achieving their goals, one day at a time. People need to be determined to reach their goals – even when things are difficult.

6. Explain to the class that they will be playing a game where they will get to help Dorothy, the Tinman, the Lion, and the Scarecrow reach the "Land of Oz," by following the Yellow Brick Road. Responsible goal setting will add bricks to the road, while irresponsible behaviors will take bricks away from the road.

7. Divide the class into four teams – the Dorothy Team, the Tinman Team, the Lion Team, and the Scarecrow Team. Explain that the four teams are competing to get to the "Land of Oz."

Ga

Grade
PK - 2

Materials
- Yellow pap   .o copy the "bricks'   .9)
- Copy of the Yellow Brick Road Cards (pg.90-91)
- Copy of Dorothy, Tinman, Scarecrow, and Lion (pg.92)
- Copy of "Land of Oz" cards (pg.93)

Time Needed
Approximately 30 minutes

Skills Covered
- Goal Setting
- Decision-Making Skills
- Study Skills

Grade Levels

PK - 2

Materials

- Yellow paper on which to copy the "bricks" (pg.89)
- Copy of the Yellow Brick Road Cards (pg.90-91)
- Copy of Dorothy, Tinman, Scarecrow, and Lion (pg.92)
- Copy of "Land of Oz" cards (pg.93)

Time Needed

Approximately 30 minutes

Skills Covered

- Goal Setting
- Decision-Making Skills
- Study Skills

Yellow Brick Road

Pre-Game Directions continued...

8. Explain to the class that the teams will take turns choosing Yellow Brick Road Cards and will get to either add or take away bricks from the road according to the card. The first team to have enough bricks to reach the "Land of Oz" wins the game.

Game Directions

1. Player from the Dorothy Team picks a Yellow Brick Road Card and either adds or takes away bricks according to the card.
   *Hint – make sure the first round of cards adds bricks to the road.

2. Player from the Tinman Team has next turn.

3. Player from the Lion Team has next turn.

4. Player from the Scarecrow Team has next turn.

5. Game continues with each team taking a turn until one of the teams reaches the "Land of Oz."

Follow-Up

- What are the goals of Dorothy, the Tinman, the Lion, and the Scarecrow in the story, "The Wizard of Oz?" How do they go about reaching their goals?
- Describe a goal that you wanted to reach. How did you go about reaching this goal?
- What are some goals that you would like to achieve in the future? What are some ways that you can help yourself achieve these goals?

Yellow Brick Road Cards

You need to learn your Math facts. You practice with flashcards every day.

Add 2 Bricks

You want to play football. You practice running and throwing the ball with your friends during recess.

Add 2 Bricks

You want to get a new skateboard. You save your allowance and ask your parents if you can do extra chores in order to earn more money.

Add 3 Bricks

You ask your parents' permission to stay up late and watch a movie. You do all your homework and chores, and get your backpack ready for school before the movie begins.

Add 3 Bricks

You want to make some new friends. You ask people if they want to play with you. You are polite and nice to others.

Add 2 Bricks

You want to have healthy teeth. However, you do not brush your teeth every night.

Take Away 1 Brick

You want to bring your lunch to school tomorrow. You pack it at night.

Add 2 Bricks

You want to play baseball. You get bored practicing, so you go watch television instead.

Take Away 1 Brick

You want to learn how to draw. You get frustrated because your drawings are not good enough. You give up and decide that you will never be a good artist.

Take Away 1 Brick

You want to get a dog. You show your mother that you can be responsible by doing all your chores and by getting ready for school on time.

Add 2 Bricks

You want to buy lunch on days that the school serves pizza. You look at the lunch menu and tell your dad the days that you would like to buy pizza.

Add 2 Bricks

You want to be a better singer. You get frustrated and decide that you will never sound better. You quit practicing and watch television instead.

Take Away 1 Brick

You want to be a better runner. You get really tired running so you go watch movies instead.

Take Away 1 Brick

You want to be a better basketball player. You practice shooting hoops and you practice with your friends.

Add 2 Bricks

You want to learn how to cook. You ask your mom if you can help her fix dinner a few nights a week. You even clean the kitchen.

Add 3 Bricks

Yellow Brick Road Cards

You want to be a better reader. You get really frustrated with reading, so you quit and decide to go play outside.

Take Away 1 Brick

You want to learn how to sew. You ask your mom for a needle, thread, buttons, and scraps of material. You practice sewing the buttons on the material.

Add 3 Bricks

You want to learn how to do cartwheels better. They are really hard to do, so you decide to give up and work on a puzzle.

Take Away 1 Brick

You want to finish a huge puzzle at your house. You set up a little table for your puzzle in your room. You work on it a little each night.

Add 3 Bricks

You have a spelling test on Friday. You wait until Friday morning to look at the words.

Take Away 1 Brick

You have to read a book for homework. You wait until bedtime to open up your book.

Take Away 1 Brick

You have a test in three days. Each night, you use some time to study for your test. The night before, you finish studying and review.

Add 3 Bricks

You have to return your library books tomorrow. You wait until it is time to catch the bus to start looking for the books.

Take Away 1 Brick

You want to make sure you do not miss the bus. You get up as soon as your mom tells you to get up. You get dressed right away.

Add 1 Brick

You want to be prepared for school. You pack your backpack before you go to bed. You make sure everything you need for school is in your backpack.

Add 2 Bricks

You want to be responsible. You make sure you have everything you need for your homework before you leave school.

Add 1 Brick

You want to be a better dancer. Someone laughs at the way you dance, so you quit dancing.

Take Away 1 Brick

You want to be prepared. You bring at least two sharpened pencils to class every day.

Add 1 Brick

You want to be responsible. You write down all your homework before you leave school.

Add 1 Brick

You want to get a good grade. You check your work before turning it in to your teacher.

Add 1 Brick

Land of   OZ

Land of   OZ

Land of   OZ
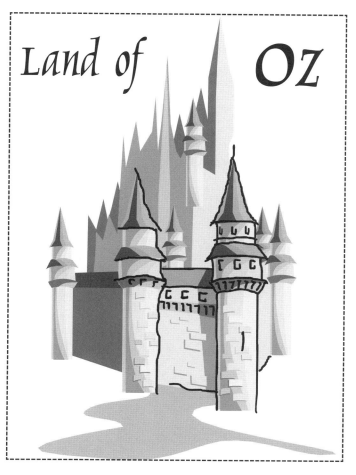

Land of   OZ
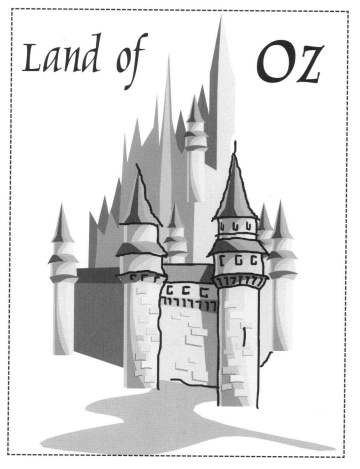

Dear Parents/Guardians,

Today, your child participated in a classroom guidance game entitled, "Yellow-Brick Road." The objective of this game was to teach students the importance of setting goals and planning ways to reach these goals. We talked about the Scarecrow, the Lion, the Tinman and Dorothy in "The Wizard of Oz." We talked about how each one of these characters wanted something – a brain, courage, a heart, and to go home. We talked about how we all have things that we want to achieve.

In this game, students were divided into four teams – the Scarecrow, the Lion, the Tinman, and Dorothy - and competed to get to the "Land of Oz." Players were given scenarios that described behaviors that help people reach their goals or inhibit them from reaching their goals. Teams added or subtracted bricks from the yellow brick road to Oz.

At home tonight, you can talk to your child about some goals that he/she wants to achieve. You can help your child develop a plan that will help him/her reach these goals.

Thanks for your support,

The Three Pigs

Grade Levels

PK - 2

Materials

- Two Bricks
- Small Pile of Straw or Shredded Paper
- Small Pile of Twigs
- Copy of Decision Cards (pp.97-98)

Time Needed

Approximately 30 minutes

Skills Covered

- Decision-Making Skills
- Responsibility

Introduction

Students have a lot of fun deciding whether a decision is a good decision – like the pig who built his house with bricks, or a bad decision – like the pigs who built their houses with straw and sticks.

Pre-Game Directions

1. In front of the classroom, place bricks on one side of the room.

2. In front of the classroom, put twigs and paper/straw together on the opposite side of the room.

3. Copy and cut apart Decision Cards.

4. Tell the class a short version of the story of "The Three Pigs." One such version follows.

> Once upon a time there were three pigs who lived together with their mother. The pigs decided to go out into the world on their own. The first pig was impatient and built his house out of the first thing he found, which was straw. The second pig was also in a big hurry to build his house. He found some twigs and quickly built a house of twigs. The third pig took his time and found some bricks. He did a good job of building his house of bricks. One day a wolf came along, in search of some little pigs to eat for his lunch. First, he came to the house of straw. He stood outside the house and demanded that the pig come out. The pig refused so the wolf huffed and puffed and blew his house down. Away the little pig ran to his brother's house of twigs. And lo and behold, the wolf ended up at that house too. He demanded that they come out of the house, but they refused so he huffed and puffed and blew the twig house down. Luckily, the little pigs escaped to their brother's house of bricks. And what do you know – that wolf ended up outside of the brick house too! He demanded that those pigs come out of the house and they refused. He huffed and puffed and huffed and puffed, but he could not blow that house down. He finally gave up and went back to his mom's house and ate a hot dog instead of one of the little pigs!

5. Talk to the class about how the third little pig made a very good decision by taking his time and building a house of bricks. The first two pigs were impatient and did not take their time. Therefore, the straw and twig houses were not good decisions because the wolf easily blew these houses down.

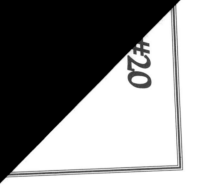

#20

Shredded Paper
• Small Pile of Twigs
• Copy of Decision Cards
(pp.97-98)

Time Needed

Approximately 30 minutes

Skills Covered

• Decision-Making Skills
• Responsibility

The Three Pigs

Pre-Game Directions continued...

6. Explain to the class that we, like the little pigs, are faced with decisions every day. We can make good decisions or we can make not-so-good decisions. Often, the good decisions are hard to make and sometimes take more work and time. However, the end result of a good decision is much better because it is a decision that makes us happy, as well as others.

7. Tell the class that we will be playing a game where we have to decide if a decision is a good decision or a not-so-good decision. Students will get to place not-so-good decisions in the pile of straw and twigs. Students will get to place good decisions on the pile of bricks.

Game Directions

1. Each student has a turn to pick a card from the Decision Cards.

2. Each student must decide if the card describes a good decision or a not-so-good decision. Students can place the good decisions on the pile of bricks and the not-so-good decisions on the pile of straw and twigs.

3. Game continues as time allows.

Follow-Up

• What do you think about the wolf's decisions in the story? Which of his decisions were good decisions? Which were not-so-good decisions?
• Why do you think the first two pigs were in such a big hurry to build their houses? Are you ever in a hurry to get something done? What are some problems that may occur when people rush through something?
• What do you think about the pig in the house of bricks who let his two brother pigs come and stay with him?

Decision Cards

Your sister took your CD, so you punched her.

Your mom asked you to clean your room. Instead you played in your room.

You did your homework as soon as you got home from school.

You packed your backpack before you went to bed.

Someone in your class needs a red crayon so you loan her one of your red crayons.

You listened to the teacher's directions before beginning your work.

Someone in your class forgot his pencil at home so you loaned him one of yours.

You did all your homework.

You did not want to do your math homework, so instead you played a game.

Your friend was mean to you so you called her some names.

You told Jamie that he could not be on your team because he is not a fast runner.

You told Carrie that she could not be in your special club.

Your mom told you to pick out your clothes for tomorrow. You watched a movie instead.

Your teacher wrote your mom a note. You left it at school and did not give it to your mom.

Your parents told you to go to bed at 8:00. You stayed up reading until 9:30.

Decision Cards

You are having trouble with your math, so you practiced using flashcards.

You could not read some of the words on your morning work. You asked your teacher to help you.

You cleaned up your room without your parents having to ask you to clean it up.

You wanted some candy at the store, but you did not have enough money so you put the candy in your pocket.

You helped your mom clean up the kitchen.

A boy made a face at you so you tattled on him.

A girl in your class was sitting by herself at lunch, so you asked her if she wanted to sit beside you.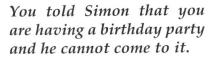

You told Simon that you are having a birthday party and he cannot come to it.

You brought an extra pencil to school in case you lost or broke your other pencil.

Someone in your class needed a glue stick, but you would not let her borrow yours.

Someone teased a boy in your class about his shoes. Everyone laughed at him so you laughed at him too.

A new student came to your class. You asked her if she wanted to play with you at recess.

Your mom told you to go to bed so you immediately put on your pajamas, brushed your teeth and got in bed.

You remembered to return your library book on time to the library.

You brought home everything you need to do your homework.

Dear Parents/Guardians,

Today, your child participated in a classroom guidance game entitled, "The Three Pigs." The objective of this game was to teach students the importance of making good decisions. We talked about how the three pigs built different houses – one straw, one stick, and one brick. The brick house took longer to make, but ended up being a better decision because the wolf could not blow it down.

In this game, students picked scenario cards that described good decisions or not-so-good decisions. Students determined what kind of decision was on each card and placed good decision cards on a pile of bricks and not-so-good decision cards on a pile of sticks and straw.

At home tonight, you can talk to your child about the importance of making good decisions, even when it might be quicker and easier to make a not-so-good decision.

Thanks for your support,

Game #21

Grade Levels

PK - 2

Materials

• Copy of Each of the Goal Setting Categories (pp.103-105)

Time Needed

Approximately 30 minutes

Skills Covered

• Goal Setting

• Decision-Making Skills

• Study Skills

Goal Setting Long Jump

Introduction

Students have a great time demonstrating their knowledge of goal achievement by way of the long jump.

Pre-Game Directions

1. If possible, laminate the Goal Setting Categories for durability.

2. Place each of the Goal Setting Categories on the floor, in a vertical line.

3. Ask the class if they know the meaning of the word "goal." Explain that the word "goal" means something that people want to achieve. Go over some common goals that elementary school students may have such as: playing soccer, being a better reader, being a better artist, getting good grades, staying out of trouble, etc.

4. Ask the students to think of some goals they would like to achieve. Ask the students to think of some steps they should take in order to achieve these goals. For example, if they want to be better soccer players, they should run, practice kicking the ball, and practice soccer with their friends or on a team.

5. Ask the students if they are good jumpers. Have them all practice jumping up and down - they love this! Explain that they will be playing a game where they will have to jump out as far as they can. Have them practice jumping forwards and backwards.

6. Show the students the line of Goal Setting Categories. Talk about each of these categories and discuss goals that students can set for themselves for each of the categories. Some examples follow:

    • **Sports** – Students may set goals such as learning to hit the ball in baseball, learning to dribble in basketball, running faster, learning how to play soccer, etc.

    • **Reading** – Students may set goals such as learning how to read, reading more, reading more difficult books, learning more vocabulary, working on spelling, etc.

    • **Math** – Students may set goals such as learning addition facts, learning multiplication facts, learning how to multiply, learning to add better, etc.

    • **School Behavior** – Students may set goals such as being a better listener, doing a better job of staying seated, doing a better job of following directions, etc.

Goal Setting Long Jump

Game #21

Grade Levels
PK - 2

Materials
• Copy of Each of the Goal Setting Categories (pp.103-105)

Time Needed
Approximately 30 minutes

Skills Covered
• Goal Setting
• Decision-Making Skills
• Study Skills

Pre-Game Directions continued...

- **Home Behavior** – Students may set goals such as doing a better job of doing chores, doing a better job of obeying parents, doing a better job of doing homework, etc.

- **Arts and Crafts** – Students may set goals such as learning how to sew, learning how to cook, being a better painter, etc.

- **Games** – Students may set goals such as learning how to play checkers, being a better video game player, having better sportsmanship behaviors, etc.

- **Friendship** - Students may set goals such as doing a better job at sharing, doing a better job at being nice to everyone, doing a better job at listening instead of talking, etc.

- **Family** – Students may set goals such as doing a better job at talking to grandparents on the phone, sharing with brothers and sisters, helping parents around the house, etc.

- **Organization** – Students may set goals such as doing a better job at packing their backpacks, doing a better job of bringing everything home they need for their homework, making sure they keep their desks neat, etc.

7. Explain that the class will be divided into two teams. Each student will get the opportunity to jump as far as they can to one of the ten categories. Each of the categories will be worth ten, nine, eight, seven, six, five, four, three, two, or one point, depending on the order of the categories for that round. The categories furthest away will be worth the most points. For example, the first round could look like this:

Sports	**10 points**
Reading	**9 points**
Math	**8 points**
School Behavior	**7 points**
Home Behavior	**6 points**
Arts and Crafts	**5 points**
Games	**4 points**
Friendship	**3 points**
Family	**2 points**
Organization	**1 point**

The student will then have to answer the following question,

- **"What goal would you like to achieve in this category?"**
- **"List some of the steps you can take in order to achieve this goal."**

Students cannot repeat goals that other students have used as their answers. The student's team will receive the number of points the category was worth for that round.

Game #21

Grade Levels

PK - 2

Materials

• Copy of Each of the Goal Setting Categories (pp.103-105)

Time Needed

Approximately 30 minutes

Skills Covered

• Goal Setting

• Decision-Making Skills

• Study Skills

Goal Setting Long Jump

Pre-Game Directions continued...

8. After one player from each team takes a turn, one round will be complete. After each round, the order of the categories will be changed. Therefore, the point value for each category will change after each round.

Game Directions

1. Divide the class into two teams.

2. Player from Team A stands at the bottom of the line of categories. Player jumps out. Player must answer the following questions regarding the nearest category:

   • **"What goal would you like to achieve in this category?"**
   • **"List some of the steps you can take in order to achieve this goal."**

3. Team A gets number of points category was worth in this round.

4. Player from Team B proceeds as Team A.

5. Change order of categories.

6. Next player from Team A proceeds. Points are given. Next player from Team B proceeds. Points are given. Change order of categories.

7. Game continues as time allows. Team with most points wins game.

Follow-Up

• What was the most difficult goal to set and explain in this game?
• What are some difficult goals to set and achieve in real life?
• What happens when we set goals for ourselves, but do not think of steps we need to take in order to reach these goals?

SPORTS

READING

MATH

SCHOOL BEHAVIOR

FRIENDSHIP

FAMILY

GAMES

HOME BEHAVIOR

Dear Parents/Guardians,

Today, your child participated in a classroom guidance game entitled, "Goal Setting Long Jump." The objective of this game was to teach students the importance of setting and achieving goals. We talked about goals that we can set for ourselves in the areas of: sports, arts and crafts, math, reading, organization, school behaviors, home behaviors, games, family, and friendship.

In this game, students jumped to one of these goal areas that were placed on the floor. Depending on which area the students landed, students had to talk about a goal they wanted to reach in this area and a way to achieve it. For example, if he/she landed on "Sports," he/she might say, "I want to be a better basketball player. In order to do so, I need to practice shooting baskets at home."

At home tonight, you can encourage your child to talk about different goals and ways to reach these goals in each of the areas from our game.

Thanks for your support,

Career Bingo

Introduction

This is a fun game that non-readers as well as readers will enjoy! At the same time, students will learn about different careers.

Pre-Game Directions

1. Copy and cut out Career Bingo Boards.

2. Briefly go over each of the following careers with the class:

• **Nurse**	• **Firefighter**	• **Postal Worker**
• **Police Officer**	• **Teacher**	• **Florist**
• **Mechanic**	• **Doctor**	• **Nurse**
• **Plumber**	• **Cook**	• **Artist**
• **Author**	• **Farmer**	• **Hairdresser**

Game Directions

1. Give each student a Career Bingo Board.

2. For younger students, call out the names of the careers and help the students find the pictures of those careers on their bingo cards. For older students, you can describe the careers to the students and have them guess the names of the careers before placing their markers on the pictures.

3. When a student has four markers in a row, he/she can call "Bingo."

4. Continue playing as time allows.

Follow-Up

- Name some of the careers that were new to you in our game.
- What careers interest you?
- What are some things that you should be doing now and in the future so that you can learn more about careers?
- What are some things that you should be doing now and in the future that will help train you for different careers?

Grade Levels

PK - 2

Materials

- Copies of Career Bingo Boards (pp.108-120)
- Bingo Markers (Buttons, Dried Beans, Pasta, Etc.)

Time Needed

Approximately 30 minutes

Skills Covered

- Career Information & Exploration

Career Bingo

Career Bingo

Career Bingo

Career Bingo

Career Bingo

Career Bingo

Career Bingo

Career Bingo

Career Bingo

Career Bingo

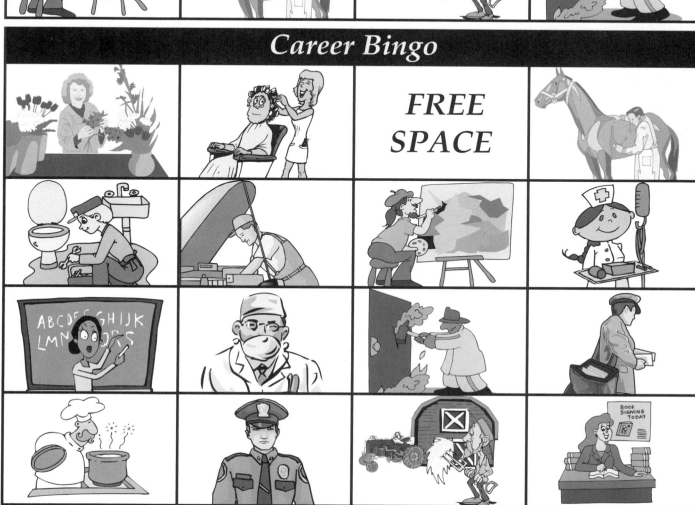

Career Bingo

Career Bingo

Career Bingo

Career Bingo

Career Bingo

Career Bingo

Career Bingo

Career Bingo

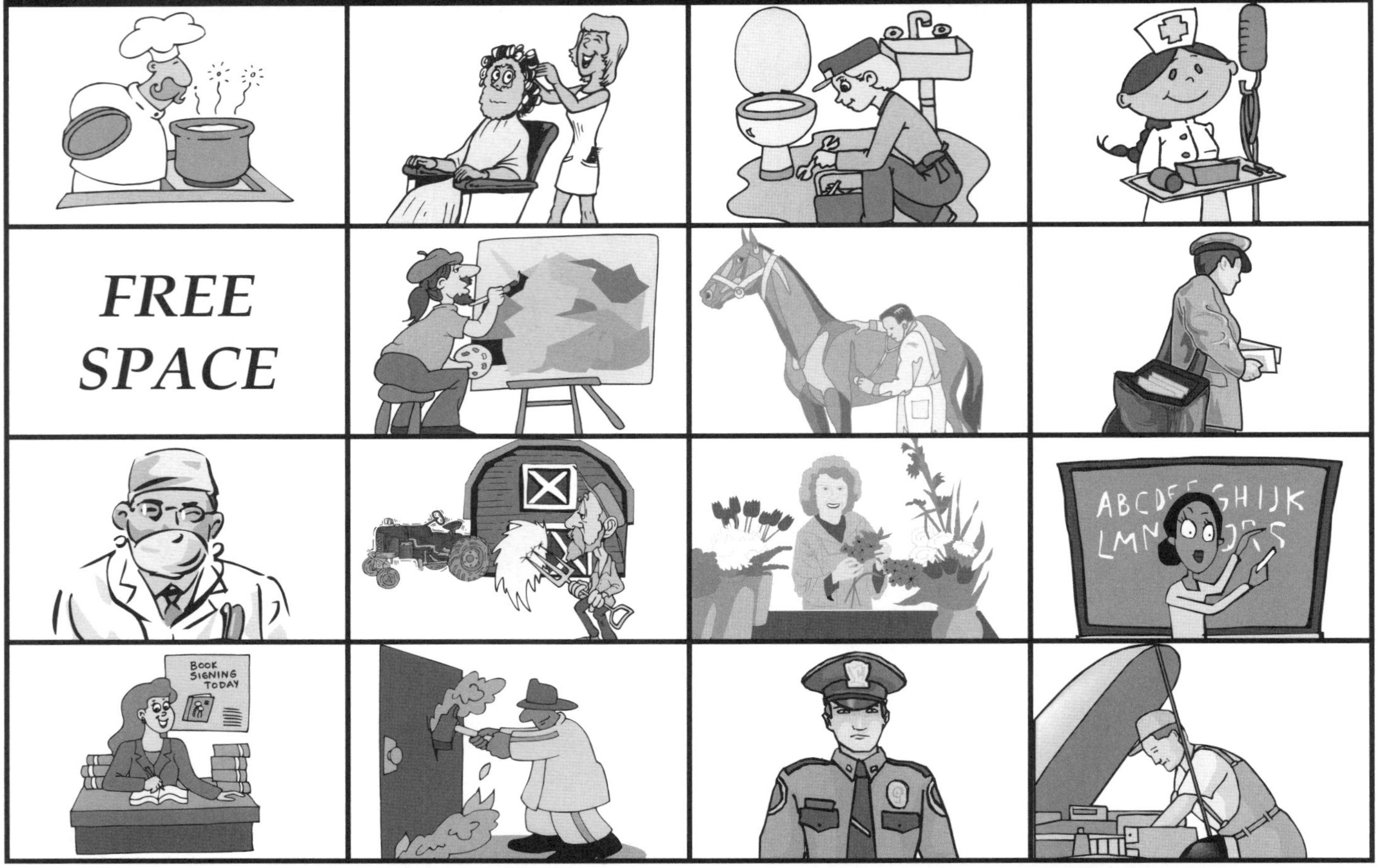

Career Bingo

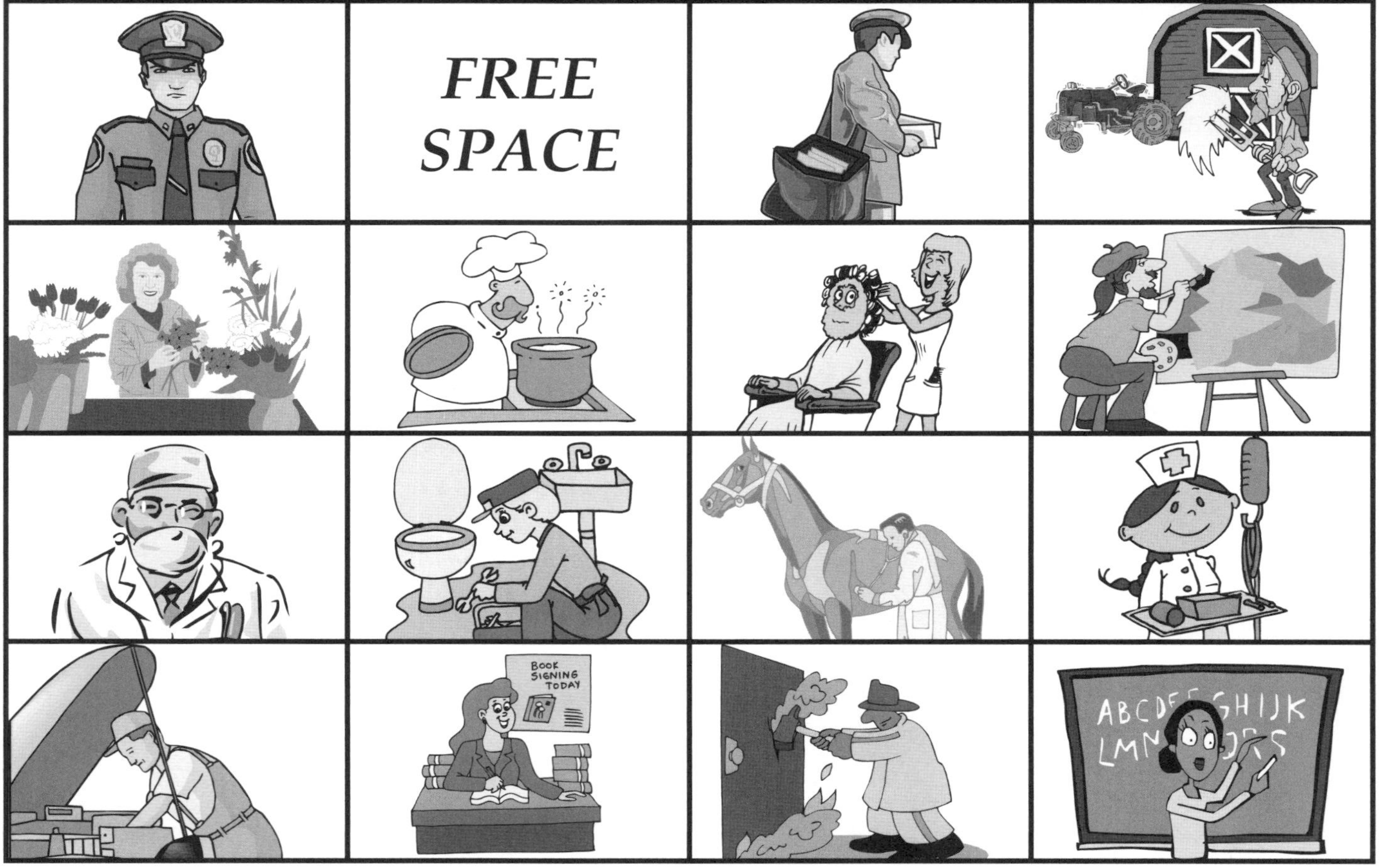

Dear Parents/Guardians,

Today, your child participated in a classroom guidance game entitled, "Career Bingo." The objective of this game was to introduce students to many different careers such as a nurse, firefighter, postal worker, police officer, teacher, florist, mechanic, doctor, nurse, plumber, cook, artist, author, farmer, and hairdresser.

In this game, students played Bingo with boards that included pictures of the careers that we discussed.

At home tonight, you can review these careers with your child. You can help your child think of people that you know that have these careers or places that these people work. Your child can talk to you about careers that interest him/her.

Thanks for your support,

Game #23

Grade Levels
PK - 2

Materials
- Markers or Crayons
- Whiteboard or Large Pieces of Butcher Paper
- Copy of Goal Setting Cards (pp.124-125)

Time Needed
Approximately 30 minutes

Skills Covered
- Goal Setting
- Achieving Goals

Draw Your Goals!

Introduction
This game is really fun for students to get a chance to learn about effective study skills, while getting a chance to draw! This is a great game for even those students who have difficulty reading and writing!

Pre-Game Directions

1. Copy and cut out the Goal Setting Cards.

2. Ask the students to define the word "goal." Explain that a goal is something that you want to reach, something you want to do or achieve. For example, a goal could be to learn how to play basketball, do a better job at reading, be a better friend, etc.

3. Ask students about different ways to set goals. For example, if a goal is to complete homework, what things can be done to reach this goal? Answers such as a desk, pencils, paper, notebook, book, light, etc. are good answers. If the goal is to be a better soccer player, students could answer by saying things such as: running, exercising, playing with friends, eating healthy, getting enough sleep, etc.

4. Go over the Goal Setting Cards to help the students become more familiar with the objects they will be drawing.

5. Explain to the class that we will be playing a game about goal setting behaviors. The class will be divided into two teams.

6. Each student will choose a card and then will have a turn to try to draw a picture that depicts and describes this card. The team will have two minutes to guess the object drawn by the student.

7. The team gets one point for guessing the goal setting object.

8. The team gets an additional point if the player can explain how this goal setting object could be used to achieve a goal. For example, if the student draws a picture of a pencil and his/her team correctly guesses, he/she could then explain that he/she could use a pencil to complete classwork. This explanation would give the team an additional point.

Draw Your Goals!

Game Directions

1. Player from Team A picks a card and has two minutes to draw a picture that depicts goal setting object while Team A guesses.

2. Team A gets one point if they guess the goal setting object in the allotted two minutes.

3. Team A gets an additional point if the player can explain a way to use the picture to achieve a goal.

4. Team B proceeds as Team A.

5. Continue game as time allows.

6. Team with most points wins the game.

Game Variation

- Students can play a game of charades with the goal setting cards.

Grade Levels

PK - 2

Materials

- Markers or Crayons
- Whiteboard or Large Pieces of Butcher Paper
- Copy of Goal Setting Cards (pp.124-125)

Time Needed

Approximately 30 minutes

Skills Covered

- Goal Setting
- Achieving Goals

Goal Setting Cards

Pencil	Paper	Math Facts
Books	Basketball	Dancing
Soccer	Baseball	Running
Sleeping	Eating Breakfast	Swimming
Playing Piano	Singing	Playing

Goal Setting Cards

Jumping Rope	Playing Cards	Exercise
Scissors	Reading	School
Notebook	Crayons	Glue
Friends	Desk	Backpack
Games	Paintbrush	Gymnastics

Dear Parents/Guardians,

Today, your child participated in a classroom guidance game entitled, "Draw Your Goals." The objective of this game was to explore student goals and ways to achieve these goals.

In this game, students were divided into two teams. Players picked cards with words describing goals or ways to achieve goals. Players had to silently draw pictures and their teams had to correctly guess the words on the cards for one point. The teams could earn an additional point if the players described a way that the word on their card could be used to achieve a goal. For example, one of our cards was the word, "desk." After guessing the word "desk" from the pictures drawn by the player, the player could then say something like, "I use my desk to do my homework so that my homework is neat."

At home tonight, you can encourage your child to continue to try and achieve his/her goals. You can help your child plan ways to make sure that he/she does not lose sight of or give up on his/her goals.

Thanks for your support,

The Tortoise and the Hare

Game #24

Grade Levels
PK - 2

Materials
- Copy of Tortoise and Hare Cards (pp.129-130)
- Copy of Picture of Hare (pg.131)
- Copy of Picture of Tortoise (pg.131)

Time Needed
Approximately 30 minutes

Skills Covered
- Decision-Making Skills
- Goal Setting
- Achieving Goals

Introduction

This game helps students understand the importance of planning in order to achieve goals. This is a fantastic game for younger students, even preschoolers. Students are told the story of "The Tortoise and the Hare" and then play a game where they decide if decisions are slow and well-planned, like the decisions of the tortoise or whether they are quick and impulsive, like the decisions of the hare.

Pre-Game Directions

1. Tape the picture of hare to one side of wall/board in front of room.

2. Tape the picture of tortoise to opposite side of wall/board in front of room.

3. Tell a revised, summary story of Aesop's Fable, "The Tortoise and the Hare." One such story follows:

   Once upon a time, there was a tortoise and a hare. The tortoise was a smart, well-planned little fellow. He took his time and always did his best in everything he did. Sometimes, it took him a little longer to complete things than others – but it did not matter because he always did a great job. On the other hand, the hare was a fast-moving, quick to think and act guy. He could get things done very quickly, but the results were not always so great – things were messy, disorganized and incorrect. The hare was always bragging to the tortoise about how fast he was. One day, he was bragging and bragging about how fast he could run. He said that he could win any race out there. He kept teasing the poor tortoise and telling him that he was slow. Finally, the tortoise was just completely sick of the whole thing and agreed to race the hare. The hare and the tortoise stood at the starting line. The hare just stood there and bragged about how fast he could run and how he could beat anyone out there. When the race started, the hare was still standing there bragging. The tortoise started his race and took his time. He kept his eyes on the goal, which was the end of the race and kept working towards it. The hare danced all around, spent some time picking flowers, and took a little rest. And lo and behold, the tortoise won the race!

4. Talk to the students about how hard the tortoise worked to win the race. Talk about how the hare did not achieve his goal because he wasted his time, bragging and doing other things.

5. Ask the students about some goals and ways they can achieve these goals. Help them think of slow, steady, and well-planned steps they can use to achieve these goals.

Game #24

Grade Levels

PK - 2

Materials

- Copy of Tortoise and Hare Cards (pp.129-130)
- Copy of Picture of Hare (pg.131)
- Copy of Picture of Tortoise (pg.131)

Time Needed

Approximately 30 minutes

Skills Covered

- Decision-Making Skills
- Goal Setting
- Achieving Goals

The Tortoise and the Hare

Pre-Game Directions continued...

6. Tell the class that they will be participating in a game where they will have to decide if someone is using slow, steady, well-planned steps (like the tortoise) or if they are using impulsive, poorly planned steps (like the hare).

7. Give the students a few examples and let them decide if the actions described are like that of the tortoise or that of the hare.

   - Say to the students, "Sarah rushed through her work and skipped a few questions. Were Sarah's actions like that of the hare or the tortoise?" Talk about why Sarah's actions were impulsive and poorly planned like the hare's behaviors.
   - Say to the students, "Tommy took his time taking his test. He checked his answers before turning it in. Were Tommy's actions like that of the hare or the tortoise?" Talk about why Tommy's actions were well-planned and careful like that of the tortoise.

8. Explain to the students that each person will get the opportunity to pick a Tortoise and Hare Card. The student will decide if the actions on the card describe responsible, slow, well-planned actions like that of the tortoise, or impulsive, poorly planned behaviors like that of the hare. The student will place the card under the picture of the hare or the tortoise, depending on the actions described on the card.

Game Directions

1. Each student will be given the opportunity to pick a Tortoise and Hare Card.

2. Each student must decide whether the actions described on the card are like that of the Hare (quick, impulsive, poorly planned) or like that of the Tortoise (slow, well planned) and place the card under the picture of either the Hare or the Tortoise.

3. Play game as time allows.

Follow-Up

- What was the goal of the tortoise?
- How did the tortoise reach his goal and win the race?
- What can happen if you are in a hurry when you are doing your homework?
- What are some tasks at school and at home that require planning and patience in order to achieve success?

Page 128

Copyright YouthLight, Inc.

Tortoise and Hare Cards

Jorge checked his backpack before he went to school.

Sarah took her time doing her work.

Tina looked at each answer before circling the correct one.

Tico was in a big hurry to finish his work so he just scribbled on his paper.

Portia waited patiently for her turn to get off the bus.

Jamison listened to all the directions before beginning his work.

Patricia really wanted to say something in class so she got out of her seat, waved her hand, and called her teacher's name.

Gloria started painting a picture before listening to the directions.

Gracie used her best handwriting to complete her work.

Damien was in a hurry to get on the bus so he ran, but tripped up and fell down.

When it was time for lunch, Deidre waited until her teacher called her table to get in the lunch line.

Tibor raised his hand and waited for his teacher to call on him.

When it was time for storytime, Carlos ran over to the carpet and knocked someone down.

Katelyn was in a hurry to eat her snack and ran to her desk, but she tripped up and dropped her cookies.

Sunita rushed through her work so she could finish first.

Tortoise and Hare Cards

Jimmy thought about what he wanted to draw before he began his artwork.

Megan waited patiently in the lunch line. She did not shove or push her tray or others around her.

On her test, Shelby circled any answers she wanted – she just wanted to finish it.

Maria quietly stood in her place in the line for water.

Jordan started using her glue before her teacher told her what to do with it, which ruined her picture.

Lola cleaned her room as soon as her mom asked her to do it.

Tommy waited patiently for his turn to throw the ball.

Billy made sure he had his backpack and lunchbox packed before he went to bed.

Sam completed his homework as soon as he got home from school.

Derek picked out the clothes he wanted to wear the night before school.

Antonio was in such a hurry to get on the swings that he knocked someone down.

Suzie did not get crayons when they were passed out so she started yelling her teacher's name over and over again.

Skylar was playing games instead of getting ready for school and she missed the bus.

Harry cleaned his room and pushed everything under his bed.

Jared was really hungry so he ran to the front of the lunch line and was pushing everyone out of his way.

Dear Parents/Guardians,

Today, your child participated in a classroom guidance game entitled, "The Tortoise and the Hare." The objective of this game was to teach students the importance of planning and taking their time.

A version of Aesop's fable, "The Tortoise and the Hare" was read to the students. We talked about how the Hare did not plan his actions and how the Tortoise did not lose sight of his goal to win the race.

In this game, students picked cards that described either well-planned actions or poorly planned actions. Students had to place the cards under a picture of the Hare – if the actions were poorly planned or under a picture of the Tortoise – if the actions were well-planned.

At home tonight, you can talk to your child about some of his/her decisions that have been poorly planned and did not go well and some of his/her decisions that have been well-planned and were successful. You can encourage your child to continue making good decisions.

Thanks for your support,

Four Corners Study Skills

Game #25

Grade Levels
PK - 2

Materials
• Copy of Four Corners Study Skills Questions (pg.135)

Time Needed
Approximately 30 minutes

Skills Covered
• Study Skills

• Responsibility

Introduction

This game requires no setup! It is fun, easy, fast moving, and requires the brain power of your students! It's easy for you and fun for them — a winner!

Pre-Game Directions

1. Talk to the class about the importance of study skills. Ask them to list some study skills they use.

2. Explain to the class that they will be participating in a game where they will have the opportunity to think about their favorite study skills.

Game Directions

1. Pick one person to be the "Super Study Buddy." This person will need to stand outside the classroom door.

2. Ask four of the remaining class members to name one thing they put in their backpacks every day. For example, the four answers might be: pencil, paper, notebook, and crayons.

3. Designate one of these items to each of the four corners of room. For example, the four corners could be the pencil corner, the paper corner, the notebook corner, and the crayon corner.

4. Tell the students to go to the corner of the room that represents their favorite school supply.

5. Step outside and ask the Super Study Buddy the same question, "What is one thing you put in your backpack every day?" The Super Study Buddy will enter the classroom and answer the question. If he/she says any of the four answers designated to a room corner, everyone in that corner is "moved to the Honor Society." For example, if he/she says, "pencil," everyone in the "pencil corner" is "moved to the Honor Society."

6. The students who are "moved to the Honor Society" sit in their seats.

7. A new Super Study Buddy is selected and stands outside the door.

8. The seated students are asked the next question, "What is one thing you should do when taking a test?" Four of their answers are each designated to a corner of the room. For example, their answers could be: check answers, take time, read the directions, and read the whole question and all answers.

Game #25

Grade Levels

PK - 2

Materials

• Copy of Four Corners Study Skills Questions (pg.135)

Time Needed

Approximately 30 minutes

Skills Covered

• Study Skills

• Responsibility

Four Corners Study Skills

Game Directions continued...

9. All students who are not "moved to the Honor Society" should go to the corner of the room that is designated for the answer that is the most important to them.

10. The Super Study Buddy is then asked the same question, "What is one thing you should do when taking a test?" He/she answers this question in the classroom. If the answer is the same as any of the four corners, the students in that corner are "moved to the Honor Society" and should sit in their seats.

11. Repeat steps 7-10 until one student remains.

12. After first game is over, game can be played again as time allows. Study Skills Questions can be repeated.

Follow-Up

• Ask the class one of the Four Corners Study Skills Questions. Choose four answers supplied by the class. Ask the students to raise their hands to indicate their choice of the four answers. Create a bar graph that shows the students' choices of answers.

Four Corners Study Skills Questions

1. What is one thing you should put in your backpack every day?

2. What are some things you should do when you are taking a test?

3. Where should you study?

4. What are some important study skills to use when your teacher is teaching you something new?

5. What should you do if you are having trouble with reading?

6. What are some things you should have in your desk?

7. How should you act when your teacher is talking?

8. What are some things you should do as soon as you get to school?

9. What should you do if you are having trouble in math?

10. What should you remember to take home from school?

Dear Parents/Guardians,

Today, your child participated in a classroom guidance game entitled, "Four Corners Study Skills." The objective of this game was to share and review study skills that help ensure academic success.

In this game, one student was picked as the "Super Study Buddy." This person was asked a question about study skills in the hall, away from the other students. The students were then asked the same question and had to go to one of the corners of the room depending on their answers. After the Super Study Buddy announced his/her answer, all students who had the same answer were "moved to the Honor Society," and sat back in their seats. The game continued until only one student remained.

At home tonight, you can talk to your child about his/her strengths and weaknesses in study skills. You can encourage your child to continue strengthening skills of organization, completing classwork, completing home-work, and being prepared.

Thanks for your support,

Chapter 4

Respect

Games in this chapter concentrate on anti-bullying, getting along with others, conflict resolution, tattling, teamwork, and safety for grades 2-6.

26

ide Levels

2-6

Materials

- 6 o......nt colored small balls (3 . 4 for each team)
- Copy of Positive Ball Compliments (pg.140)

Time Needed

Approximately 30 minutes

Skills Covered

- Getting Along With Others
- Positive Communication
- Social Skills

Positive Ball

Introduction

This is a fun, interactive game that lets students move around and practice respectful things to say.

Pre-Game Directions

1. Explain to class that they will be participating in a game today where they will practice respectful, positive things to say to one another.

2. Talk about the importance of compliments and saying things to encourage one another. Ask students to give an example of a time someone encouraged or complimented them. Talk about how it feels for someone to say positive things to you.

3. Explain that the class will be divided into two teams. Students will be playing a game where the object will be to keep different balls in the air as long as possible.

4. If the balls are dropped, if negative comments are made, if students get out of their seats, or if the balls are thrown in the wrong order, the team is "out" and the opposing team gets a point.

Game Directions

1. Divide class into two teams.

2. Give a student on Team A and Team B a ball (Ball #1). Explain that Ball #1 will be used for positive comments. The first student from each team will say teammate's name, say a positive comment about that person and throw the ball to him/her.

3. The students who catch the ball will each say another student's name, say a positive comment about that person, and throw the ball to him/her.

4. Steps #1 and #2 are repeated until all students on each team have had a chance to catch the ball. After everyone has had a turn, continue to throw Ball #1 in the same order (to the same person).

5. Next, introduce a second, different colored ball (Ball #2) to a person on each team. Before throwing this ball, the student holding the ball will need to say someone's name and say something that he/she is good at doing. The person who catches the ball will need to call someone's name and say something that he/she is good at doing. Ball #2 will continue to be thrown until all students have had a turn. After everyone has had a turn, continue to throw ball #2 in the same order (to the same person).

Positive Ball

Grade Levels

2-6

Materials

- 6 or 8 different colored small balls (3 or 4 for each team)
- Copy of Positive Ball Compliments (pg.140)

Time Needed

Approximately 30 minutes

Skills Covered

- Getting Along With Others
- Positive Communication
- Social Skills

Game Directions continued...

6. Continue to introduce new, different colored balls. The object is to have a few different balls being thrown at the same time.

7. Each time the ball is dropped, someone gets out of his/her seat, a negative comment is made, or the ball is thrown in the wrong order, the opposing team gets a point and game is started over.

Game Variation

- Instead of saying a compliment to the person to whom the ball is thrown, students must ask a question that helps get to know that person better. For example, students can ask questions like, "What is your favorite song?"

ositive Ball Compliments

1. [Say] something positive about the person.

2. Say something that the person is good at doing.

3. Say a subject in which the person works hard.

4. Say something the person likes to do outside of school.

5. Say something you like about the person's clothes.

6. Say something the person does that is respectful.

7. Say something the person does that is responsible.

8. Say something the person does that is fun.

9. Say something the person does that is nice.

10. Say something the person does that is helpful.

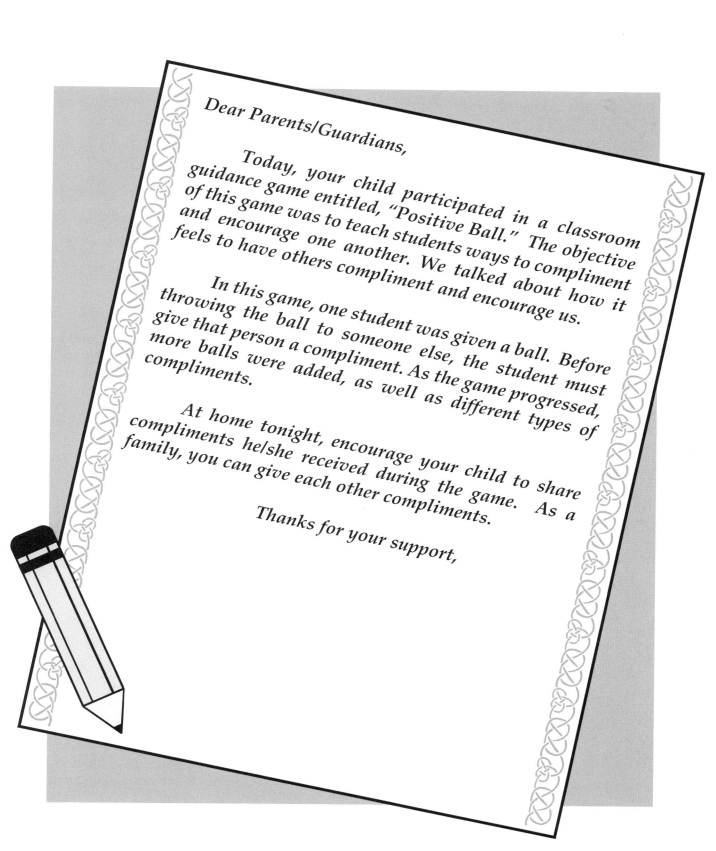

Dear Parents/Guardians,

Today, your child participated in a classroom guidance game entitled, "Positive Ball." The objective of this game was to teach students ways to compliment and encourage one another. We talked about how it feels to have others compliment and encourage us.

In this game, one student was given a ball. Before throwing the ball to someone else, the student must give that person a compliment. As the game progressed, more balls were added, as well as different types of compliments.

At home tonight, encourage your child to share compliments he/she received during the game. As a family, you can give each other compliments.

Thanks for your support,

Game #27

Grade Levels
2-6

Materials
• Small Basketball Hoop or Bucket / Basket

• Small Ball

• Copy of No-Bully Basketball Scenarios (pg.144-145)

• Copy of Questions To Ask Yourself (pg.146)

Time Needed
Approximately 30 minutes

Skills Covered
• No-Bully Behaviors

• Getting Along With Others

• Conflict Resolution

No-Bully Basketball

Introduction
What a fun way to teach behaviors that help prevent bullying! This game has been a big hit from everyone that has tried it!

Pre-Game Directions

1. Tape copy of Questions To Ask Yourself in the front of the room.

2. Place basketball hoop (or bucket/basket) in the front of the room.

3. Copy and cut out No-Bully Basketball Scenarios.

4. Explain to class that you will be working on ways for students to get along with others.

5. Ask students to define "bullying." Explain that bullying behaviors are those that threaten to harm or physically harm others. Bullying behaviors also include continually harassing others. If someone is being bullied, he/she needs to ask an adult for help. Talk about some adults that can help students – parents, aunts, uncles, grandparents, teachers, principals, counselors, ministers, doctors, policemen, etc.

6. Go over Questions to Ask Yourself. Example situations for each question follow.

   • "If someone is hitting you in the bathroom, what should you do?" Students should pick #1 (Ask an adult for help) because someone is being harmed and bullied.

   • "If someone makes a face at you, what should you do?" Students should pick #2 (Ignore the person) because this is a behavior that is easy to ignore.

   • "If your friend hurts your feelings, what should you do?" Students should pick #3 (Talk about it with your friend).

7. Go over the last question of the Questions to Ask Yourself – "Is there anything I can do to avoid this from happening in the future?" Have students answer this question for each of the situations described above.

8. Explain that the class will be playing a game of "No-Bully Basketball" where teams compete by appropriately answering ways to respond to different bullying and annoying situations. Each student will have the opportunity to pick a situation card. The student must answer the Questions to Ask Yourself for each situation. If correctly answered, the team gets two points, except for the 3-pointer questions (which are labeled as such). The team can receive an additional two points if a student throws the ball into the basket/bucket or hoop.

No-Bully Basketball

Grade Levels
2-6

Materials
- Small Basketball Hoop or Bucket / Basket
- Small Ball
- Copy of No-Bully Basketball Scenarios (pg.144-145)
- Copy of Questions To Ask Yourself (pg.146)

Time Needed
Approximately 30 minutes

Skills Covered
- No-Bully Behaviors
- Getting Along With Others
- Conflict Resolution

Pre-Game Directions continued...

9. Explain that points may be taken away for any unsportsman-like behaviors.

10. Divide class into two teams.

Game Directions

1. Player from Team A goes first and draws a scenario card. Team A must decide how they would act in this situation. Team A gets two points for appropriate answers, except for three pointer scenarios which award three points.

2. Player A then gets an opportunity to "shoot" the "basketball" into the "basket." The team is awarded two points for shots that land in the basket.

3. Team B proceeds as Team A.

4. Game proceeds as time allows.

5. The team with most points wins the game.

Follow-Up

- What are some behaviors that are very difficult for you to ignore? Are you able to ignore it when someone talks about your family? What can you do to prevent an argument when you are very upset or angry?
- Why do you think students are sometimes reluctant to ask an adult for help if they are being bullied or threatened?
- Write a descriptive paragraph or paper answering the following question. What do you think are the biggest conflicts that students have with one another and how can these be prevented?

No-Bully Basketball Scenario Cards

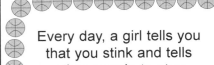 Every day, a girl tells you that you stink and tells other people to stay away from you.

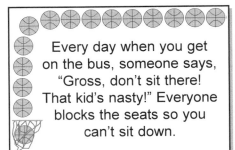 Every day when you get on the bus, someone says, "Gross, don't sit there! That kid's nasty!" Everyone blocks the seats so you can't sit down.

 Your friend told you that he heard someone talking about you.

 Someone said he is going to jump you in the bathroom.

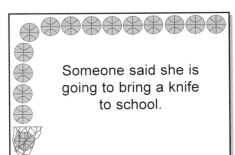 Someone said she is going to bring a knife to school.

 You heard a 5th grader threaten a 3rd grader.

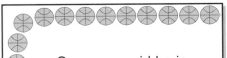 Someone talked about your mother.

 Someone said that you're gross.

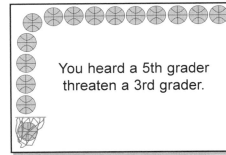 Someone said that your clothes look like they came from the dump.

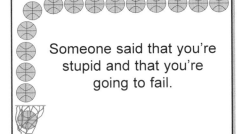 Someone said that you're stupid and that you're going to fail.

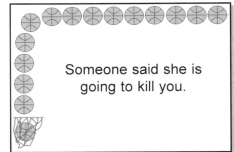 Someone said she is going to kill you.

 Someone said he is going to hurt himself.

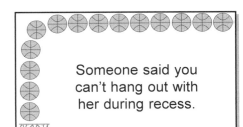 Someone said you can't hang out with her during recess.

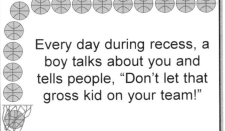 Every day during recess, a boy talks about you and tells people, "Don't let that gross kid on your team!"

 Someone made you give her your snack money.

No-Bully Basketball Scenario Cards

Your friend said that people don't like you anymore.

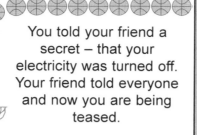
You told your friend a secret – that your electricity was turned off. Your friend told everyone and now you are being teased.

You and your friend are horseplaying. Things get a little rough and your friend really starts hurting you.

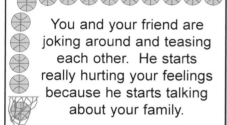
You and your friend are joking around and teasing each other. He starts really hurting your feelings because he starts talking about your family.

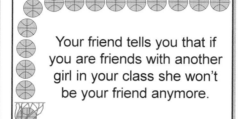
Your friend tells you that if you are friends with another girl in your class she won't be your friend anymore.

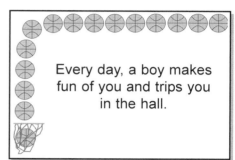
Every day, a boy makes fun of you and trips you in the hall.

Bonus "3-Pointer" Questions

What can I do?

How would I feel if I were this person?

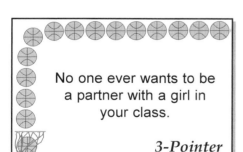
No one ever wants to be a partner with a girl in your class.

3-Pointer

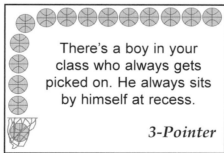
There's a boy in your class who always gets picked on. He always sits by himself at recess.

3-Pointer

A girl in your class sits by herself during lunch every day.

3-Pointer

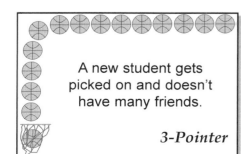
A new student gets picked on and doesn't have many friends.

3-Pointer

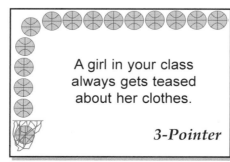
A girl in your class always gets teased about her clothes.

3-Pointer

A boy in your class never gets picked for a team.

3-Pointer

No-Bully Basketball Questions

First, Ask Yourself:

1. Is someone being bullied or hurt? Should I ask an adult for help? Who is an adult that I can tell?

2. Should I ignore the problem?

3. Should I talk to the person with whom I am having problems?

Next, Ask Yourself:

4. Is there anything I can do to avoid this problem from happening in the future?

BONUS "3-Pointer" Questions

Ask Yourself:

1. What can I do?

2. How would I feel if I were this person?

Dear Parents/Guardians,

Today, your child participated in a classroom guidance game entitled, "No-Bully Basketball." The objective of this game was to teach students behaviors that do not encourage bullying and things to do if someone is being bullied. We defined bullying as behaviors that harass, harm, or threaten others.

In this game, students were divided into two teams. Players chose scenario cards that described potential problem situations. Players decided if the situations needed adult help or if they could handle it on their own. For situations that needed adult help (someone being bullied or threatened), players named an adult that they would tell. For situations that did not need adult help (minor teasing or hurt feelings), players described how to resolve the conflicts. Teams received points for correctly answered questions and for successfully making a basket!

At home tonight, you can talk to your child about the importance of telling an adult if someone is being bullied.

Thanks for your support,

Game #28

Grade Levels

2-6

Materials

- 3 buckets or boxes for 1st, 2nd, and 3rd base
- Small Ball
- Marker for Home Plate
- Copy of Safety Baseball Question Cards (pp.150-151)

Time Needed

Approximately 30 minutes

Skills Covered

- Safety
- Respect for Self and Others

Safety Baseball

Introduction

Students have a great time learning about and practicing rules of safety while playing a competitive, indoor game of baseball!

Pre-Game Directions

1. Copy and cut out Safety Baseball Question Cards.

2. Place home plate in front of room.

3. Place the three buckets/boxes as 1st, 2nd, and 3rd base. 1st base should be placed relatively close to home plate.

4. Explain to class that they will be participating in a fun game of indoor baseball where they will be able to show off their knowledge of important safety rules.

5. Ask students to share some school safety rules, some bus safety rules, and some home safety rules.

6. Ask students to explain why these rules are important.

7. Divide class into two teams.

Game Directions

1. Each team will send a student to "bat." The batter will have 3 attempts to throw the ball into the 1st, 2nd, or 3rd base. After 3 tries, the batter is "out" if the ball does not land in a base box.

2. If a student gets the ball into a base box, he/she has the opportunity to draw a safety card and correctly answer the question. His/her team can assist with the answer. If answered correctly, he/she (Player A) goes to the base in which the ball landed (ex. if the ball landed in the 2nd base box, he/she gets to go to 2nd base). The team will get 1 point for getting on base.

3. Next player (Player B) will go to "bat." If the ball lands in 1st base box and safety question is answered correctly, Player B will go to 1st base and Player A will advance to 3rd base. The team gets a point for Player B getting on base.

4. If Player B had landed the ball in the 2nd or 3rd base box and correctly answered the safety question, he/she would move to that base and Player A would advance 2 bases (if the ball landed in 2nd base box) or 3 bases (if the ball landed in 3rd base box). The team gets one point every time a player gets on base.

5. When a player reaches home plate, the team gets an additional point.

Safety Baseball

Game #28

Grade Levels

2-6

Materials

- 3 buckets or boxes for 1st, 2nd, and 3rd base
- Small Ball
- Marker for Home Plate
- Copy of Safety Baseball Question Cards (pp.150-151)

Time Needed

Approximately 30 minutes

Skills Covered

- Safety
- Respect for Self and Others

Game Directions continued...

6. Each team member will take a turn until the team gets three outs or if every member of the team has had a turn, at which point it automatically becomes the other team's turn.

7. The game continues as time allows. The team with the most points wins the game.

Follow-Up

- Do you think it is difficult to tell an adult if one of your friends is doing something dangerous? Why or why not? Why is it important to tell an adult even if you are worried that your friend will be angry with you?
- Which safety rule do you think is the most important at school or at home? Why?
- Write a persuasive paragraph or essay about one safety rule that should be changed or added at your school.

Safety Baseball Question Cards

Name 3 reasons people should not drink alcohol.

Pretend that your house is on fire. You've gone to a neighbor's house to call 911. What are 3 important things you need to tell the 911 operator?

Name 3 reasons people should not smoke.

What would you do if your best friend brought a lighter to school?

You and your friend are hanging out. Your friend takes out some matches. What should you do?

You have a baby sister. Name three things that you should make sure are out of the baby's reach.

Your older brother has cigarettes in his backpack. What will you do?

If there are guns in your house, where should they be kept for safekeeping?

Name three reasons why people should not do drugs.

What should you do if you know that someone is hurting one of your friends?

Name three people you could tell if someone hurts you.

Your friend tells you that someone has touched him inappropriately and asks you not to tell anyone. What should you do or say?

Name three things you should do in order to be safe when riding your bike.

What could happen if people run in the hallways?

Name three appropriate behaviors for the bus.

Safety Baseball Question Cards

Name three inappropriate behaviors on the bus.

Why is it important to use safe behaviors on the bus?

What is the first thing you should put on after you sit down in a car?

Your friend has some cigarettes and wants you to smoke with her. What will you do or say?

Your mother or father is very, very sick. You call 911. What are three important things to tell the 911 operator?

Your friend realizes that he accidentally brought a pocketknife to school. He asks you not to tell anyone. What should you do or say?

Someone knocks on your door and your parents aren't home. What should you do?

What should you do if your clothes are on fire?

What should you do if your house is on fire?

What should you do if a stranger says he has lost his dog and needs you to help him find it?

What should you do if someone you talked to on the internet asks you to meet him?

What should you do if someone sends you inappropriate messages or pictures through the internet?

What should you do if someone you talked to on the internet asks you to send her pictures of you?

What should you do if your friend wants to get his dad's gun out to show you?

What should you do if your friend wants you to go swimming with her while her parents are not home?

Dear Parents/Guardians,

Today, your child participated in a classroom guidance game entitled, "Safety Baseball." The objective of this game was to teach and review rules of safety at home and at school. We talked about the importance of obeying these rules for everyone's protection from harm.

In this game, the class was divided into two teams. Players picked question cards that asked questions about safe behaviors at school and at home. If answered correctly, players were then given three chances to throw a ball into one of three buckets (1st, 2nd, or 3rd base). Players advanced to the base/bucket in which their ball landed. Teams accumulated points for all players who landed on a base or reached home plate.

At home tonight, you can review safety information with your child. For example, you can practice calling emergency services. Your child will need to know his/her address, phone number, his/her full name, and the full name of parents/guardians.

Thanks for your support,

Citizenship Football

Game #29

Grade Levels

2-6

Materials

- Copy of Football Field (pg.154)
- Copy of Goal Post (pg.155)
- Copy of Football Players (pg.154)
- Die
- Copy of Citizenship Football Question Cards (pp.156-157)
- Tape or Two Paper Clips
- Small Football / Other Ball

Time Needed

Approximately 30 minutes

Skills Covered

- Respect for Self, Others, and Environment
- Citizenship

Introduction

This game is great for students to practice respect for others as well as the world around them while playing a fun, indoor game of football.

Pre-Game Directions

1. Copy and cut out Citizenship Football Question Cards.

2. Tape copy of football field in front of room.

3. Tape copy of goal post in front of room.

4. Clip or tape football players to the 50-yard line.

5. Talk to class about the meaning of the word citizenship. Explain that citizenship means our commitment to our community and our world. Tell the class that they will be playing a game with questions that will focus on ways to be better citizens.

6. Divide class into two teams.

7. Flip coin to see which team goes first.

Game Directions

1. Player A from Team A picks a card. If correctly answered, Player A gets to roll the die to determine how many yards Team A gets to advance away from the 50-yard line, towards a touchdown. If the die rolled is a 1-2, player advances 10 yards, 3-4 = 20 yards, 5-6 = 30 yards. Place paper football player for Team A in correct place on football field.

2. Player B from Team B proceeds likewise.

3. First team to score a touchdown gets 6 points. This team also gets an opportunity to score an extra point if the next player is able to throw the small football and hit the goal post on the wall.

4. Game continues as time allows. Team with most points wins.

Follow-Up

- Name some famous people who are good citizens. What do they do to make the world a better place?
- Name some people in your community who are good citizens. What do they do to make the world a better place?
- Write a descriptive paragraph or paper describing the person you think is the best citizen in your class. How is he/she a good citizen? What does he/she do to make our world a better place?

TOUCHDOWN

10 20 30 40 50 40 30 20 10

✂ Cut along dotted lines.

10 20 30 40 50 40 30 20 10

TOUCHDOWN

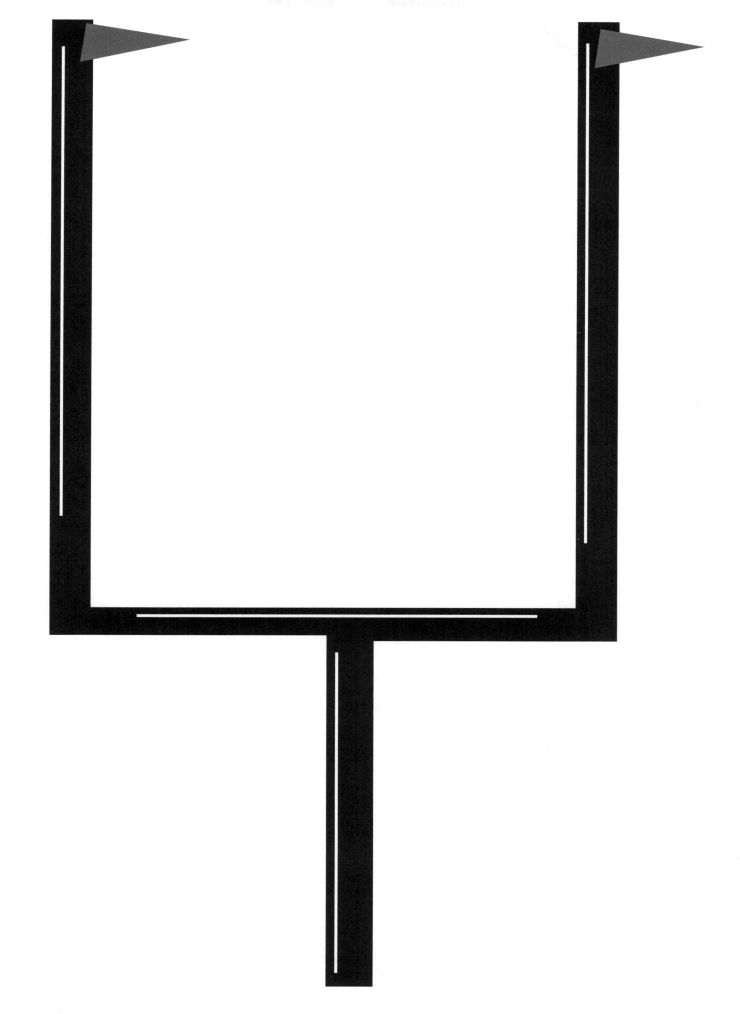

Citizenship Football Question Cards

What should you do with aluminum cans?

What should you do with glass bottles?

What should you do with old newspapers?

What should you do if you see trash on the floor?

What should you do if someone drops their books on the floor?

What should you do if you find a bracelet in the bathroom?

What should you do if someone is looking for his notebook?

What should you do if you find a library book in the hall?

How should you care for library books?

Name 3 ways you can help care for the earth.

Name 3 ways you can help care for your classmates.

What should you do with trash in the car?

Name something that you love about living in your town or city.

Name 3 ways you can help care for your school.

What should you do if someone drops a water bottle and it spills everywhere?
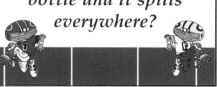

Citizenship Football Question Cards

What should you do if someone in your class can't find his pencil?

What should you do if someone is sitting alone at lunch every day?

What should you do when a new student comes to your school?

What should you do if someone sits alone every day during recess?

What should you do if no one wants to be someone's friend in your class?

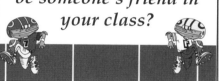

What should you do if everyone always picks the same student last during games?

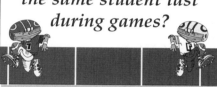

What should you do if no one ever wants to be one person's partner in class?

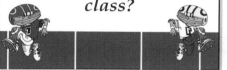

How should you care for something that you borrow from one of your friends?

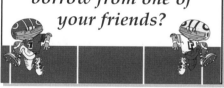

What should you do if you lose a CD you borrowed from your friend?

How should you treat the computers at school?

How should you treat school property?

Name 3 ways you can help care for your home.

Name 3 ways you can help care for your family.

Name 3 ways you can be a good example for younger students.

Name 3 things you love about your school.

Dear Parents/Guardians,

Today, your child participated in a classroom guidance game entitled, "Citizenship Football." The objective of this game was to teach students about the importance of respect for others, our community, and our world. We talked about people that we know that are good citizens and have contributed to our world.

In this game, students were divided into two teams. Players picked question cards about ways to be a good citizen. If answered correctly, teams advanced their football players 10, 20, or 30 yards on our football field game board.

At home tonight, you can encourage your child to talk about ways that he/she would like our world to improve or change. You can talk about ways that your child can help make these changes happen.

Thanks for your support,

Class Collage

Grade Levels

2-6

Materials

- Large Piece of Poster Board or Butcher Paper
- Index Card for Each Student
- Tape
- Markers, Crayons, and/or Colored Pencils

Time Needed

Approximately 30 minutes

Skills Covered

- Getting Along With Others
- Positive Communication
- Social Skills

Introduction

Not only does this game allow students to share something positive about themselves, it also helps students think about others. The result of this game is a colorful collage that can be displayed to remind students to be proud of themselves and others.

Pre-Game Directions

1. Tape large piece of poster board or butcher paper in front of room.

2. Explain to the class that they will be participating in a game where they will get to "show off" interesting things about themselves. Explain that each student has talents and unique characteristics. Explain that everyone should be proud of these talents and characteristics.

3. Explain that students should embrace their differences because these characteristics are what make each of us special, individual, and unique.

Game Directions

1. Give each student an index card.

2. Ask the students to silently write down the coolest thing about themselves on the lined side of the index card. Make sure that no one else sees what each student has written.

3. Once completed, collect and shuffle the index cards.

4. Read (aloud) each card. Allow three students to guess who wrote each card before telling class who wrote the card.

5. After all cards have been read, return cards to students. Instruct them to decorate the opposite side of the card, illustrating the coolest thing about them.

6. When completed, tape the index cards to the large paper to make a class collage.

Follow-Up

- What is the greatest thing you learned about someone in your class?
- Why do you think it is important for people to be proud of their individual characteristics and talents?
- Why do you think people sometimes hide their uniqueness?
- Do you think that people your age try to be like everyone else or do you think they like to be different from others?

Dear Parents/Guardians,

Today, your child participated in a classroom guidance game entitled, "Class Collage." The objective of this game was to teach students respect for differences in others. Before beginning the game, we talked about how we all have interesting and unique characteristics and talents. We talked about the importance of respecting everyone.

In this game, students wrote down one unique characteristic about themselves on an index card. The students guessed who wrote each card, thus learning some interesting things about each other. Students decorated the opposite sides of their cards with a picture of their uniqueness. The cards were put together to create a class collage.

At home tonight, you can talk to your child about why people often try to be like others and are afraid to be themselves. You can encourage your child to be proud of his/her individual traits and to be brave enough to be different.

Thanks for your support,

Conflict Resolution Ring Toss

Grade Levels

2-6

Materials

- 3 Cardboard Paper Towel Holders
- 3 Plastic Lids
  (like those found on coffee cans)
- Shoebox
- Tape
- Scissors
- Copy of Conflict Resolution Ring Toss Cards (pp.163-164)

Time Needed

Approximately 30 minutes

Skills Covered

- Getting Along With Others
- Conflict Resolution
- Social Skills

Introduction

This game is easy to make! Simple household items can be used to create an exciting game of ring toss. Teams compete for points by tossing the rings and answering questions about getting along with one another.

Pre-Game Directions

1. Cut out 3 cardboard squares from the shoebox (approx. 5"x5").

2. Fasten (with tape) the paper towel holder to the cardboard square so that it stands upright in order to create the ring base.

3. Cut out the inner circle from the top of each of the coffee can lids in order to create the rings. Label one ring base "Appropriate Actions," the second one "Appropriate Reactions," and the third "Appropriate Follow-Up."

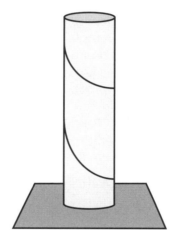

4. Copy and cut out the Conflict Resolution Ring Toss Cards.

5. Place the ring bases in front of the classroom.

6. Divide the cards into three piles: Appropriate Actions, Appropriate Reactions, and Appropriate Follow-Up.

7. Talk to the class about the difficulties of getting along with others. Explain that everyone has trouble getting along sometimes – even friends and families.

8. Explain that the class will be participating in a game and will attempt to toss rings around 3 different ring bases. The class will be divided into two teams and teams will compete for points.

9. If a ring lands around any ring bases, the team whose player threw the ring will receive one point for each ring that landed around a base.

10. The team can earn additional points by correctly answering questions that correspond with the ring bases on which the rings landed. For example, if the ring lands around the "Appropriate Actions" ring base, the player will get to choose one of the Conflict Resolution Cards labeled "Appropriate Actions." If correctly answered, the team will gain an additional point. If the ring lands around the "Appropriate Reactions" ring base, the player will choose a card labeled, "Appropriate Reactions" and so forth.

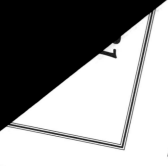

31

Levels
2-6

Materials
per Towel Holders

• 3 Plastic Lids
(like those found on coffee cans)

• Shoebox

• Tape

• Scissors

• Copy of Conflict Resolution Ring Toss Cards (pp.163-164)

Time Needed
Approximately 30 minutes

Skills Covered
• Getting Along With Others

• Conflict Resolution

• Social Skills

Conflict Resolution Ring Toss

Pre-Game Directions continued...

11. Discuss appropriate actions, reactions, and follow-up behaviors to angry situations. For an Appropriate Action example, ask the class what they should do if one of their friends is not talking to them. An appropriate action would be to ask the friend, in private, if something is wrong. An inappropriate action would be to talk about that person or get mad at that person. For an Appropriate Reaction example, ask the class what they should do if some one bumps into them and knocks their books on the floor. An appropriate reaction would be to pick up the books. An inappropriate reaction would be to push the person or throw books. For an Appropriate Follow-Up example, ask the class what they should do if someone has been playing around and teasing too much. An appropriate follow-up would be to ask the person, in private, to stop teasing. An inappropriate follow-up would be to blow up at the person.

Game Directions

1. Divide the class into two teams.

2. Player from Team A tosses the three rings.

3. Team A gets one point for each ring that lands around a ring base.

4. For each ring that lands around a ring base, player from Team A can choose a question that corresponds with that ring base. For example, if one ring lands on the Appropriate Follow-Up ring base and two rings land on the Appropriate Reaction ring base, player from Team A can pick one question from the Appropriate Follow-Up cards and two questions from the Appropriate Reaction cards.

5. Team A gets one point for each appropriate answer.

6. Team B proceeds as Team A.

5. Game continues as time allows.

6. The team with the most points wins the game.

Game Variation

• Number the ring bases #1, #2, and #3. Teams compete against one another by tossing the rings. Players get 1 point if the ring lands around the #1 ring base, 2 points if the ring lands around the #2 ring base, and 3 points if the ring lands around the #3 base. Players can get an additional 3 points on each turn if they describe an actual or fictional conflict and an appropriate reaction or appropriate follow-up.

Conflict Resolution Ring Toss Cards

Appropriate **Action**

Someone is sitting by himself at lunch.

Appropriate **Action**

Someone looks upset on your bus.

Appropriate **Action**

Your mom and dad are very angry because you disobeyed them.

Appropriate **Action**

Everyone is making fun of a student's clothes.

Appropriate **Action**

No one will ever talk to a student in your class.

Appropriate **Action**

Everyone teases and talks about a girl on your bus.

Appropriate **Action**

Someone is crying in your class.

Appropriate **Action**

Someone dropped his backpack and everything fell out.

Appropriate **Action**

Someone fell down during P.E. and everyone laughed.

Appropriate **Action**

Your brother is upset because he is grounded for getting poor grades.

Appropriate **Action**

Your mom is trying to clean and make dinner at the same time.

Appropriate **Action**

No one will pass the ball to one student on your team.

Appropriate **Action**

Someone cannot find their paper or pencils and class is beginning.

Appropriate **Action**

Your dad is doing yard work.

Appropriate **Action**

Your sister wants to borrow some of your clothes.

Conflict Resolution Ring Toss Cards

Appropriate
Reaction

Your brother borrowed your CD without asking.

Appropriate
Reaction

Someone called you a name on the bus.

Appropriate
Reaction

Someone keeps rolling her eyes at you in class.

Appropriate
Reaction

Someone talked about your mom.

Appropriate
Reaction

Someone told you that your friend was talking about you during lunch.

Appropriate
Reaction

Someone said that you are not good enough to be on his football team.

Appropriate
Reaction

Someone said that you think you can sing but you cannot.

Appropriate
Reaction

Someone said that a boy in your class wants to fight you.

Appropriate
Reaction

Someone said that you are going to fail because you are stupid.

Appropriate
Reaction

Someone said that you got your shoes from the dump.

Appropriate
Reaction

Someone said that you stink.

Appropriate
Reaction

Someone said that your hair looks nasty.

Appropriate
Reaction

Someone is having a party and said that you are not invited.

Appropriate
Reaction

Someone said that everyone is talking about how you think you know everything.

Appropriate
Reaction

Someone said that nobody wants to hang out with you anymore.

Conflict Resolution Ring Toss Cards

Appropriate Follow-Up

You and your friend had a disagreement yesterday because she has not been talking to you lately.

Appropriate Follow-Up

You and your friend were playing football and he hit you in the face.

Appropriate Follow-Up

Your mom grounded you because you did not study for your Math test and you failed it.

Appropriate Follow-Up

Your teacher punished you because you were disrespectful.

Appropriate Follow-Up

Your dad took away your game because you did not do your chores.

Appropriate Follow-Up

You and your brother got into an argument because he always gets in your business.

Appropriate Follow-Up

You are angry at your friend because you heard that he has been talking about you.

Appropriate Follow-Up

Your friend hurt your feelings because she made a negative comment about your clothes.

Appropriate Follow-Up

Your friends did not let you play basketball with them.

Appropriate Follow-Up

You and your sister got into an argument because she always takes your things without asking.

Appropriate Follow-Up

Your parents upset you because they promised to take you to the movies, but they changed their minds.

Appropriate Follow-Up

You are angry with your teacher because he accused you of something you did not do.

Appropriate Follow-Up

You are mad at the principal because he punished you and did not punish the other students who did the same thing.

Appropriate Follow-Up

You and your friend have a problem because he only hangs out with you when no one else is around.

Appropriate Follow-Up

You are upset at your mom because she punished you but did not listen to the whole story.

Dear Parents/Guardians,

Today, your child participated in a classroom guidance game entitled, "Conflict Resolution Ring Toss." The objective of this game was to help students think of their own ways to avoid and resolve conflicts. We discussed appropriate actions when we are upset, appropriate reactions when we have a conflict with someone, and appropriate ways to follow up after a conflict.

In this game, the class was divided into two teams for a game of ring toss. Depending on where the rings landed, students were asked questions that required appropriate actions, reactions or follow-up.

At home tonight, you can help your child think of different ways to avoid problems with others and ways to resolve conflicts with others.

Thanks for your support,

Conflict Skit In a Bag

Game #32

Grade Levels
2-6

Materials
- Paper Lunch Bags
  (one for each group of 3-4 students)
- 5 Different Household Items for Each Bag (sponges, apples, tacks, small toys, etc.)
- Copy of Each Conflict Challenge Cards (pg.169)
- Paper and Pencil for Each Team

Time Needed
Approximately 30 minutes

Skills Covered
- Getting Along With Others
- Conflict Resolution
- Teamwork

Introduction

This game is a lot of fun for the whole class! It requires creativity and conflict resolution skills.

Pre-Game Directions

1. Put five household items in each paper bag.

2. Put one Conflict Challenge Card in each paper bag.

3. Discuss appropriate conflict resolution skills with students. Ask students to explain how they deal (appropriately) with conflicts.

4. Give some examples of appropriate conflict resolution skills such as: talking it over, taking a break away from each other, deciding on a new plan to help avoid conflicts and apologizing. Ask students if any of these skills have helped them resolve a conflict. Encourage the students to share examples of conflict resolution skills that have worked for them.

5. Explain to the class that they will be divided into small groups of 3-4 students. Each group will be given a paper bag containing five household items and a Conflict Challenge Card. The group must create a silent skit portraying the conflict described on the card. The group must use all five household items in their skit. The team must be creative in their use of the items (for example, a fork could be portrayed as a telephone). In addition, the group must also act out the conflict resolution. The other teams must write down their guesses about the conflict and the conflict resolution portrayed in the skit.

6. Each team that correctly guesses the general idea of the conflict will receive ten points. Each team that correctly guesses the general idea of the conflict resolution will receive ten points. The performing team gets ten points if any of the other teams correctly guess the conflict and ten points if any of the other teams correctly guess the resolution.

Game Directions

1. Divide class into groups of 3-4 students.

2. Give each group a paper bag containing five household items and a Conflict Challenge Card.

3. Give groups 10-15 minutes to create their silent skits.

4. Each group will perform their skit. While the group performs, the other teams will write down their guesses about the conflicts and the conflict resolutions.

Game #32

Grade Levels

2-6

Materials

• Paper Lunch Bags
(one for each group of 3-4 students)

• 5 Different Household Items for
Each Bag (sponges, apples, tacks,
small toys, etc.)

• Copy of Each Conflict Challenge
Cards (pg.169)

• Paper and Pencil for Each Team

Time Needed

Approximately 30 minutes

Skills Covered

• Getting Along With Others

• Conflict Resolution

• Teamwork

Conflict Skit In a Bag

Game Directions continued...

5. After the skit is completed, collect the guesses from the other teams. Have one student from each team read their guesses aloud. Award 10 points for each correctly guessed conflict and 10 points for each correctly guessed resolution. The performing team gets 10 points for any correctly guessed conflicts and 10 points for any correctly guessed resolutions.

6. The team with the most points wins the game.

Game Variation

• Play game as stated above, but instruct students to create their own conflicts and conflict resolutions instead of using a Conflict Challenge Card.

Conflict Challenge Cards

Conflict

One of your friends took something out of your backpack without asking you.

Resolution

Talk it over with your friend and tell him that you need him to ask before he touches your things.

Conflict

Someone teased you because your basketball team lost the game.

Resolution

Spend some time by yourself at home drawing.

Conflict

One of your friends has been ignoring you and hanging out with other people.

Resolution

Talk it over with your friend and tell her that you miss hanging out with her.

Conflict

A friend borrowed one of your games. When she returned it, the game was scratched.

Resolution

Explain to your friend that you need her to respect your things and ask her to make sure that she takes care of borrowed items in the future.

Conflict

One of your classmates tells you that you are no good at soccer.

Resolution

Ignore your classmate and go play with someone else.

Conflict

One of your classmates told you that you could not be part of the baseball game on the playground.

Resolution

Go play basketball with one of your other friends.

Conflict

You are angry because your friend accused you of taking his CD that you did not take.

Resolution

Calmly talk it over with your friend.

Conflict

You are upset because you and your friend were teasing each other and she said some things that hurt your feelings.

Resolution

Ask your friend to not say those things to you anymore.

Conflict

You are mad because you and your brother are supposed to clean the kitchen together and he is talking and playing instead of cleaning.

Resolution

Tell your brother that the two of you will divide up the remaining kitchen tasks. Clean your half of the tasks and leave the kitchen.

Conflict

One of your friends invited two friends over to his house but did not invite you.

Resolution

Ask your friend if he wants to come to your house in a few days.

Dear Parents/Guardians,

Today, your child participated in a classroom guidance game entitled, "Conflict Skit in a Bag." The objective of this game was to help students practice ways to resolve conflicts. We talked about conflict resolution skills such as: talking it over, taking a break away from each other, deciding on a new plan to help avoid conflicts and apologizing.

In this game, students were divided into teams of 3-4 students. Each team was given a bag with five common household items and a conflict challenge card. With the bag of items, the team had to create a silent skit portraying the conflict and the resolution described on the conflict challenge card. The other teams attempted to correctly guess the conflict and the resolution.

At home tonight, you can encourage your child to talk to you about some of the most common conflicts he/she faces at school and at home. You can listen to your child and help him/her think of ways to avoid and resolve these conflicts.

Thanks for your support,

Get Along Categories

Introduction

In this game, students pick from four categories: Getting Along, Respecting Differences, Teamwork, and No-Bullying Behaviors.

Pre-Game Directions

1. Divide poster board into four columns. Label the columns: Getting Along, Respecting Differences, Teamwork, and No-Bullying Behaviors.

2. Place four index cards under each category. Tape or staple these cards in order to create four pockets under each category. These pockets will hold the Get Along Cards.

3. Label each of the four cards under each category – 10, 20, 30, and 40.

4. Copy and cut out Get Along Cards. Place the cards in the appropriate pockets. For example, place the 10 pt. Getting Along cards in the 10 pt. pocket under "Getting Along."

5. Place the board in front of the classroom.

6. Explain to the class that they will be participating in a game where they will get to show off their skills in getting along with one another.

7. Explain that they will be participating in a classroom game that concentrates on four areas: Getting Along, Respecting Differences, Teamwork, and No-Bullying Behaviors.

8. Explain that the students will be divided into teams of 3-5 students.

9. These teams will compete against one another for points in the game of Get Along Categories.

10. Explain that in general, the more points a question is worth, the more difficult that question is.

Game Directions

1. Divide the class into teams of 3-5 students. Allow teams to create names for their themselves.

2. Pick a team to go first. It is often fun to pick the first team based on something out of the ordinary. For example, the first team could be the team wearing the most red, or the team that has the most letters in their first names, etc.

3. Team A can pick any card from the pockets of the Get Along Board.

Grade Levels

2-6

Materials

- Large Piece of Poster Board
- 16 Index Cards
- Paper & Pencils for Each Team
- Tape or Stapler
- Copies of Get Along Cards (pp.173-176)
- Black Magic Marker

Time Needed

Approximately 30 minutes

Skills Covered

- No-Bullying Behaviors
- Respecting Differences
- Teamwork
- Friendship

33

aterial

• Large ____ er Board

• 16 Index Cards

• Paper & Pencils for Each Team

• Tape or Stapler

• Copies of Get Along Cards
(pp.173-176)

• Black Magic Marker

Time Needed

Approximately 30 minutes

Skills Covered

• No-Bullying Behaviors

• Respecting Differences

• Teamwork

• Friendship

Get Along Categories

Game Directions continued...

4. Read the question aloud to the class.

5. All teams must write down their answers to the question.

6. Teams will have TWO minutes to complete their answers.

7. Any team that has a correct answer will be awarded the number points that card was worth (example, a 20 pt card is worth 20 points). If a player picks a "Double It" card, the point value will be worth twice as much. For example, if the player picked a 20 pt. "Double It" card, it would be worth 40 pts.

8. The next team will choose a card.

9. Repeat Steps #4 - #7.

10. Play as time allows. The team with the most points wins the game.

Follow-Up

• What do you think the biggest problem is among people your age: respecting differences, bullying, getting along, or working together as a team? Explain your answer.

• What do you think adults can do to help people your age work out their problems?

• Write a short essay describing your strengths in the way you get along with others, your weaknesses in the way you get along with others, and strategies for continuing to improve your skills in getting along with others.

Get Along Cards - Getting Along

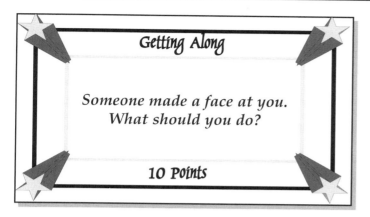

Getting Along

Someone made a face at you.
What should you do?

10 Points

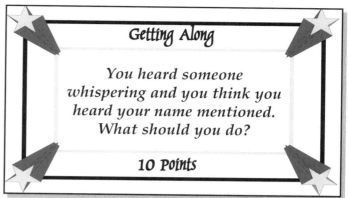

Getting Along

You heard someone
whispering and you think you
heard your name mentioned.
What should you do?

10 Points

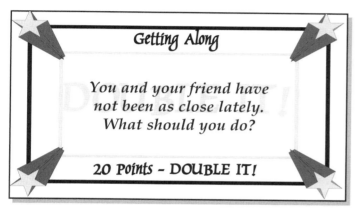

Getting Along

You and your friend have
not been as close lately.
What should you do?

20 Points - DOUBLE IT!

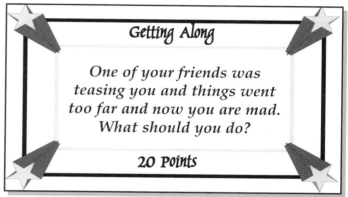

Getting Along

One of your friends was
teasing you and things went
too far and now you are mad.
What should you do?

20 Points

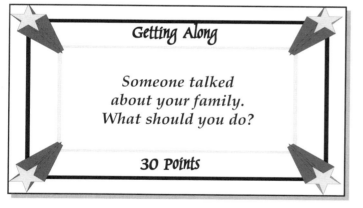

Getting Along

Someone talked
about your family.
What should you do?

30 Points

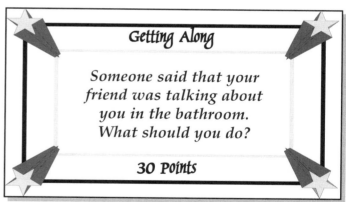

Getting Along

Someone said that your
friend was talking about
you in the bathroom.
What should you do?

30 Points

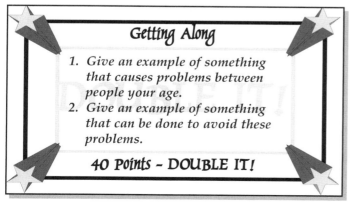

Getting Along

1. Give an example of something
   that causes problems between
   people your age.
2. Give an example of something
   that can be done to avoid these
   problems.

40 Points - DOUBLE IT!

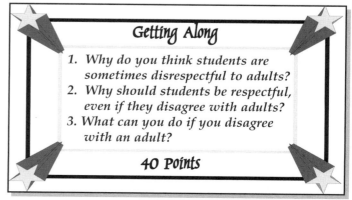

Getting Along

1. Why do you think students are
   sometimes disrespectful to adults?
2. Why should students be respectful,
   even if they disagree with adults?
3. What can you do if you disagree
   with an adult?

40 Points

Get Along Cards - Respecting Differences

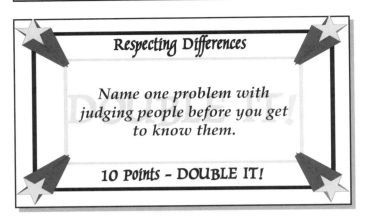

Respecting Differences

Name one problem with judging people before you get to know them.

10 Points - DOUBLE IT!

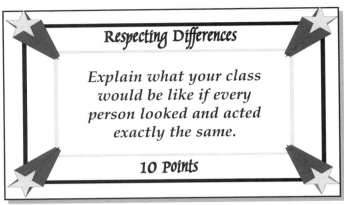

Respecting Differences

Explain what your class would be like if every person looked and acted exactly the same.

10 Points

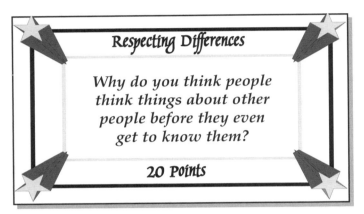

Respecting Differences

Why do you think people think things about other people before they even get to know them?

20 Points

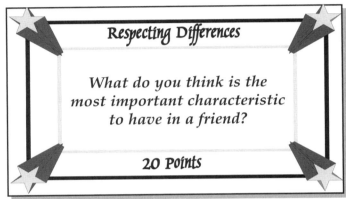

Respecting Differences

What do you think is the most important characteristic to have in a friend?

20 Points

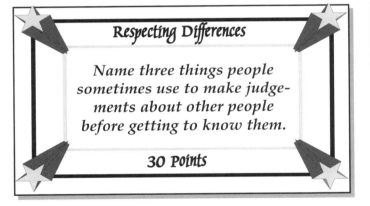

Respecting Differences

Name three things people sometimes use to make judgements about other people before getting to know them.

30 Points

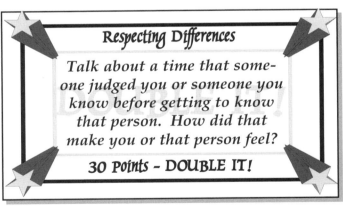

Respecting Differences

Talk about a time that someone judged you or someone you know before getting to know that person. How did that make you or that person feel?

30 Points - DOUBLE IT!

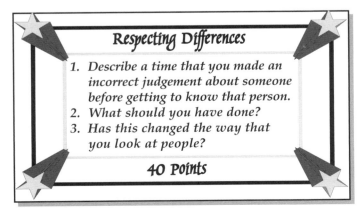

Respecting Differences

1. Describe a time that you made an incorrect judgement about someone before getting to know that person.
2. What should you have done?
3. Has this changed the way that you look at people?

40 Points

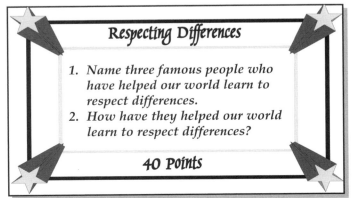

Respecting Differences

1. Name three famous people who have helped our world learn to respect differences.
2. How have they helped our world learn to respect differences?

40 Points

Get Along Cards - Teamwork

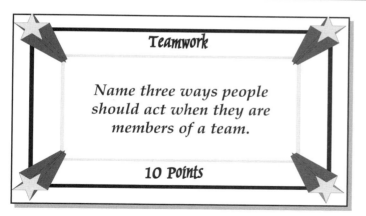

Teamwork

Name three ways people should act when they are members of a team.

10 Points

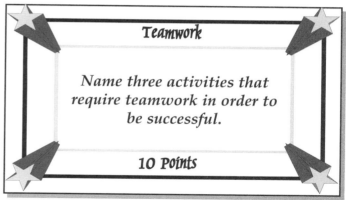

Teamwork

Name three activities that require teamwork in order to be successful.

10 Points

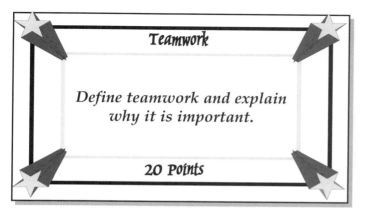

Teamwork

Define teamwork and explain why it is important.

20 Points

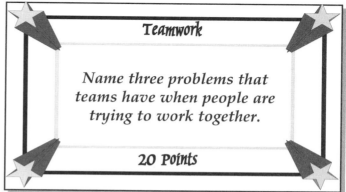

Teamwork

Name three problems that teams have when people are trying to work together.

20 Points

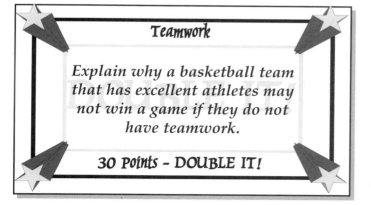

Teamwork

Explain why a basketball team that has excellent athletes may not win a game if they do not have teamwork.

30 Points - DOUBLE IT!

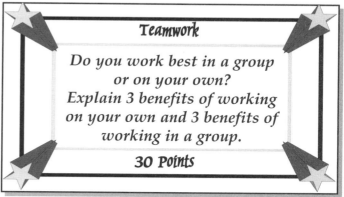

Teamwork

Do you work best in a group or on your own? Explain 3 benefits of working on your own and 3 benefits of working in a group.

30 Points

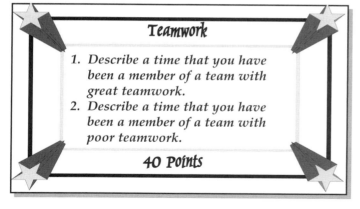

Teamwork

1. Describe a time that you have been a member of a team with great teamwork.
2. Describe a time that you have been a member of a team with poor teamwork.

40 Points

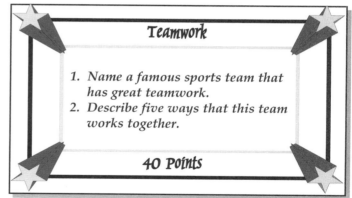

Teamwork

1. Name a famous sports team that has great teamwork.
2. Describe five ways that this team works together.

40 Points

Get Along Cards - No-Bullying Behaviors

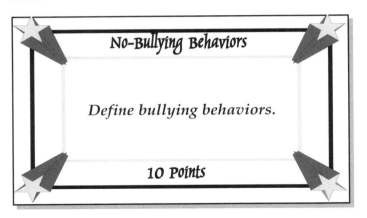

No-Bullying Behaviors

Define bullying behaviors.

10 Points

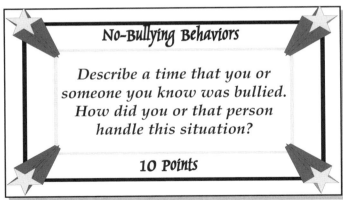

No-Bullying Behaviors

Describe a time that you or someone you know was bullied. How did you or that person handle this situation?

10 Points

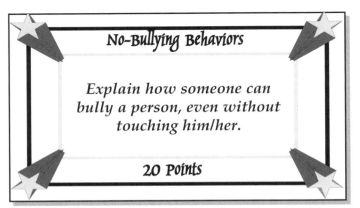

No-Bullying Behaviors

Explain how someone can bully a person, even without touching him/her.

20 Points

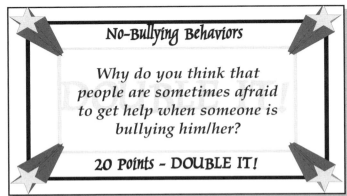

No-Bullying Behaviors

Why do you think that people are sometimes afraid to get help when someone is bullying him/her?

20 Points - DOUBLE IT!

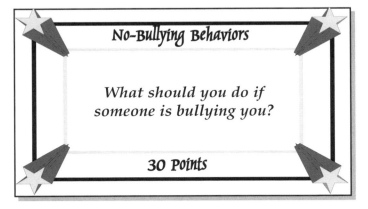

No-Bullying Behaviors

What should you do if someone is bullying you?

30 Points

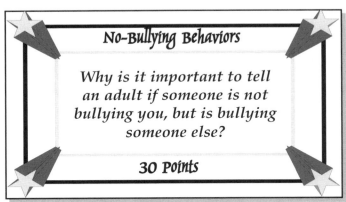

No-Bullying Behaviors

Why is it important to tell an adult if someone is not bullying you, but is bullying someone else?

30 Points

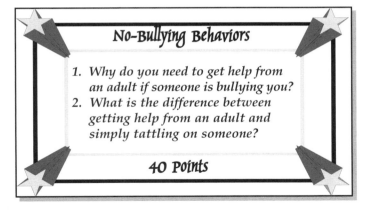

No-Bullying Behaviors

1. Why do you need to get help from an adult if someone is bullying you?
2. What is the difference between getting help from an adult and simply tattling on someone?

40 Points

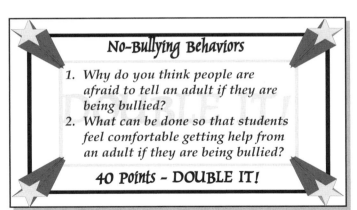

No-Bullying Behaviors

1. Why do you think people are afraid to tell an adult if they are being bullied?
2. What can be done so that students feel comfortable getting help from an adult if they are being bullied?

40 Points - DOUBLE IT!

Dear Parents/Guardians,

Today, your child participated in a classroom guidance game entitled, "Get Along Categories." The objective of this game was to teach and review the skills of friendship, respecting differences, teamwork, and no-bullying behaviors.

In this game, students were divided into two teams. Teams competed for points by answering questions in the categories of Getting Along, Respecting Differences, Teamwork, and No-Bullying Behaviors. Questions required that students explain ways to work together, respect one another, avoid problems, resolve conflicts, and to be a good friend.

At home tonight, you can encourage your child to talk about his/her strengths in the areas of friendship, respect, teamwork and getting along with others. You can ask your child about the areas that are the most difficult for him/her.

Thanks for your support,

Game #34

Materials*

- Copy of Teamwork Challenge Cards (pg.179)
- 8-10 Pieces of Poster Board, Large Pieces of Cardboard, or Large Pieces of Butcher Paper
- Long Piece of Rope for Each Team (about 6 feet)
- Blindfold for Each Student
- Masking Tape
- Metal Pots, Pans, and Metal Utensils for Each Team
- Paper and Pencils
- About 250 Blocks (50 Blocks for Each Team)

Time Needed

Approximately 30 minutes

Skills Covered

- Teamwork
- Getting Along With Others

* **The materials listed here can be used for the various Teamwork Challenges. You will not need to do all the challenges. Materials for each challenge are also listed on individual Teamwork Challenge Cards. Feel free to improvise or change these challenges.**

Teamwork Challenge

Introduction

This classroom game focuses on teamwork. Teams have to work together to win the different challenges. The team with the most points is the winner!

Pre-Game Directions

1. Talk to the class about the importance of teamwork. Explain why it is important for the success of a team and the overall positive experience of the team.

2. Talk about the problems that occur when teams do not work together – bickering, fighting, blaming, and of course, the fact that teams that do not work together do not usually win.

3. The teams will all be presented with the same Teamwork Challenges. The team that wins the challenge will be awarded 5 points. The team will receive an additional 5 points for describing the teamwork behaviors that enabled their team to win the challenge.

Game Directions

1. Divide the class into groups of 4-5 students. Allow teams to pick out names for their teams. Give them two minutes to pick out the name. Teams that pick out a name in less than two minutes, without arguing will receive five points to begin the game.

2. Pick a Teamwork Challenge Card and read it aloud to the class.

3. The team winner of the challenge receives five points. The team can receive an additional five points if they describe the teamwork behaviors that helped them win the challenge.

4. Play as time allows. Team with most points wins.

Follow-Up

- What was your favorite challenge? Why?
- What was the most difficult challenge for your team? Why?
- Which classroom team did the best job of working together? Explain how this team worked together.

Teamwork Challenge Cards

Challenge #1 – Musical Teamwork
Materials: Pots, Pans, Utensils, Pencils, and Paper

Give the pots, pans, utensils, pencils, and paper to each te

Say to the class: "You have five minutes to create words and music for a so
The team with best song wins."

Challenge #2 – Blindfold Circle
Materials: Rope and Blindfolds

Give a piece of rope to each team. Blindfold each team member.

Say to the class: "Make a circle out of the rope. The first team to create a "good" circle wins."

Challenge #3 – Stand on the Line
Materials: Masking Tape

Place 5-foot strip of masking tape on the floor for each team. Instruct each team to stand on their tape. First, take half of the tape away. Then, continue to take away pieces of tape. Team that can stand on the smallest strip of tape and hold their positions for 30 seconds wins.

Challenge #4 – Airplane
Materials: Paper

Give each team five sheets of paper.

Say to the class: "You have five minutes to create one great paper airplane. The team whose airplane flies the furthest wins this challenge."

Challenge #5 – Tall Towers
Materials: Blocks

Give each team about fifty blocks.

Say to the class: "You have five minutes to build a tower. The team with the tallest, standing tower at the end of three minutes wins this challenge."

Challenge #6 – Escape
Materials: Poster Board, Cardboard, or Butcher Paper

Give each team two pieces of poster board. Instruct all teams to stand on one side of the classroom.

Say to the class: "You and all the members of your team must get to the other side of the room. You may only stand on or touch the poster boards. You may not touch the floor or any chairs, desks or table. The first team to get to the other side of the room wins this challenge."

Dear Parents/Guardians,

Today, your child participated in a classroom guidance game entitled, "Teamwork Challenge." The objective of this game was to teach students the importance of teamwork. We talked about the benefits and the difficulties of working together as a team.

In this game, students were divided into teams of 4-5 students. Teams competed against one another to win different "teamwork challenges." Team members that worked together and supported each other helped their teams succeed.

At home tonight, you can talk to your child about the things that he/she likes and does not like about being a member of a team. You can help him/her to think of successful teams and reasons why these teams are successful.

Thanks for your support,

Chapter Five

Reflection

Games in this chapter concentrate on self-esteem, positive communication, understanding and communicating feelings, anger control, and social skills for grades 2-6.

Game #35

Materials

- Copy of Guess It Cards (pp.184-185)
- Large Piece of Poster Board or Butcher Paper
- Magic Marker

Time Needed

Approximately 30 minutes

Skills Covered

- Self-Esteem
- Positive Communication

Guess It!

Introduction

This game helps students expand their emotional vocabularies and helps students identify and describe emotions.

Pre-Game Directions

1. Copy and cut out Guess It Cards.

2. Explain to class that they will be participating in a game where they will need to guess different emotions.

3. Teams will compete with one another by guessing emotion words.

4. Explain that the class will be working in groups of 3-5 students. One person from the group will be the "Describer." The Describer will attempt to describe the words to his/her team. Five words are on each card. The team has one minute to guess the words. The team will receive one point for each correctly guessed word and an additional five points if all words on the card are correctly guessed in one minute. If the team is having difficulty guessing the word, the Describer can skip it and come back to that word. The Describer may not say the word that is to be guessed.

5. On the board, write down the 25 emotion words with the class. These include: happy, tired, unhappy, enraged, worried, excited, jealous, tired, relaxed, mad, disappointed, pleased, contented, nervous, angry, disappointed, miserable, distraught, frustrated, agitated, irritated, joyful, peaceful, furious, and calm. Make sure the class understands the meaning of each of these words. Show the class words that are synonyms (example, unhappy - sad) and words that are antonyms to one another (example, distraught – calm). Explain that using synonyms and antonyms will help the teams guess the words.

Game Directions

1. Divide class into teams of 3-5 students. Allow the teams to name themselves.

2. One player from Team A (the Describer) picks a Guess It Card.

3. The Describer must then begin describing these words to his/her team. The team must call out the words they think the describer is describing. The team has only one minute to guess all the words on the card. For the first few rounds, teams can look at the board to see the 25 emotion words that are on the cards.

Guess It!

Grade Levels

2-6

Materials

- Copy of Guess It Cards (pp.184-185)
- Large Piece of Poster Board or Butcher Paper
- Magic Marker

Time Needed

Approximately 30 minutes

Skills Covered

- Self-Esteem
- Positive Communication

4. The Describer gives a thumbs-up sign as soon as the word is guessed correctly.

5. If the describer accidentally says the word that is to be described, or a part of that word, he/she must skip that word and go to the next word. Points cannot be given if the Describer says any part of the word before it is guessed.

6. Team receives one point for each correctly guessed word and an additional five points if all words on the card are correctly guessed.

7. Each team proceeds as Team A.

8. Play as time allows. Team with most points wins the game.

Game Variation

- Players must describe each word to their teams by acting or drawing.

Guess It Cards

Happy Angry Nervous Frustrated Disappointed	Tired Enraged Calm Unhappy Frustrated
Peaceful Mad Tired Unhappy Disappointed	Disappointed Contented Calm Furious Joyful
Mad Excited Tired Peaceful Jealous	Joyful Calm Peaceful Agitated Enraged
Enraged Sad Tired Relaxed Frustrated	Nervous Disappointed Joyful Sad Unhappy
Happy Peaceful Sad Disappointed Contented	Relaxed Agitated Joyful Pleased Miserable

Guess It Cards

Excited **Happy** **Sad** **Frustrated** **Agitated**	**Irritated** **Agitated** **Sad** **Peaceful** **Mad**
Happy **Angry** **Excited** **Distraught** **Miserable**	**Excited** **Sad** **Furious** **Peaceful** **Enraged**
Furious **Tired** **Calm** **Happy** **Relaxed**	**Unhappy** **Nervous** **Sad** **Enraged** **Disappointed**
Happy **Nervous** **Calm** **Miserable** **Worried**	**Nervous** **Sad** **Enraged** **Distraught** **Jealous**
Worried **Distraught** **Unhappy** **Mad** **Excited**	**Sad** **Worried** **Joyful** **Happy** **Nervous**

Dear Parents/Guardians,

Today, your child participated in a classroom guidance game entitled, "Guess It!" The objective of this game was to help students expand their emotional vocabularies. We discussed the following emotions: happy, tired, unhappy, enraged, worried, excited, jealous, tired, relaxed, mad, disappointed, pleased, contented, nervous, angry, disappointed, miserable, distraught, frustrated, agitated, irritated, joyful, peaceful, furious, and calm.

In this game, students were divided into two teams. Players took turns describing a series of emotions to their teams. Teams had one minute to guess as many of the emotions as possible.

At home tonight, you can review each of the emotions from our game. You can encourage your child to share times he/she has felt these emotions.

Thanks for your support,

Super Prize

Game #36

Grade Levels
2-6

Materials
• Copy of Super Prize Question Cards (pp.188-189)
• Three Envelopes
• Copy of Super Prizes (pp.190-191)

Time Needed
Approximately 30 minutes

Skills Covered
• Anger Control
• Positive Communication

Introduction

In this game, based on the television show "Super Prizes," teams compete for points by answering questions about bullying and anger control.

Pre-Game Directions

1. Label the envelopes: "Prize Number One," "Prize Number Two," and "Prize Number Three."

2. Copy and cut out the Super Prize Question Cards.

3. Copy and cut out the Super Prizes. Divide these evenly and place them inside the three envelopes.

4. Tell the students that this game will concentrate on anger control. Ask students about things they do to help vent their anger and to avoid blowing up at people. Explain that everyone gets angry and that it is okay to be angry. We need to make sure that we appropriately deal with our anger. Provide the students with examples of how we can deal with our anger such as: playing outside, playing a game, having some time by yourself, talking with somebody, writing in a journal, etc.

5. Explain that the class will be divided into two teams. Players will answer questions about anger control and will be given the opportunity to receive ten points for correct answers. If the players choose to do so, they may trade their ten points and pick one of the prizes in the envelopes. The teams will be competing against each other for points.

Game Directions

1. Divide class into two teams.

2. Player from Team A picks a Super Prize Question Card. Player reads and answers the question. If correctly answered, player gets the option of receiving ten points or taking a risk and picking a prize from the envelopes marked: Prize Number One, Prize Number Two, or Prize Number Three.

3. Player from Team B proceeds as Team A.

4. Play as time allows. Team with most points wins the game.

Follow-Up

• What are some things that make you angry at school? At home?
• What are some things that help you control your anger?
• Describe a time that you did not handle your anger appropriately and explain how you should have handled it.

Super Prize Question Cards

You are upset because your mom grounded you for your report card. You had planned on going to a really fun party. What can you do to help you deal with your anger?

Name someone in your class who does a good job dealing with anger in appropriate ways. Describe how he/she deals with anger appropriately.

Describe what it physically feels like to be calm. Explain what your hands, feet, face, etc. feel like when you are calm.

What do you think is the easiest way to appropriately deal with your anger at home? Explain why you think this is the easiest way to deal with your anger at home.

What are the three things that make you the angriest? What can you do to appropriately deal with this anger?

Give an example of a time you were angry at school and a positive way you dealt with it.

Describe what it physically feels like to be angry. Explain how your head, your hands, your heart, your face, your legs, etc. feel when you are angry.

Someone said you are too much of a wimp to fight. What can you do to help you deal with your anger?

You are mad because your sister told on you and got you in trouble. What can you do to help you deal with your anger?

Give an example of a time you were angry at home and a positive way you dealt with it.

You are really frustrated because you have been trying to do your math and you cannot understand it. Everyone else seems to be doing fine. What can you do to help deal with your frustration?

You are upset at your teacher because you think he lets everyone else get away with stuff except for you. What can you do to help you deal with your feelings?

Give three reasons why you should control your anger at home.

You are mad at your friend because you think she has been talking about you behind your back. What can you do to help you deal with your anger?

You are angry with your friend because he told everybody that you like someone in your class. What can you do to help you deal with your anger?

Super Prize Question Cards

Give three reasons why you should control your anger at school.

You are disappointed because your dad said that he would come to your play at school but instead, he had to go to a meeting. What can you do to help you deal with your disappointment?

Give an example of a time when you saw someone else deal with her anger appropriately.

You are angry because your friend invited three people over to her house, but did not invite you. What can you do to help you deal with your anger?

You are angry because your cousin said he was going to trade a game with you. He took your game, but has not given you his. What can you do to help you deal with your anger?

You are upset because your friend told one of your secrets that she promised not to tell anyone. Now everyone knows and is laughing at you. What can you do to help you deal with your anger?

Explain how you feel mentally when you are calm. What thoughts do you have when you are calm? What messages do you tell yourself when you are calm? What things do you care about when you are calm?

What do you think the easiest way is to appropriately deal with anger at school? Why do you think this is the easiest way?

You are mad at your brother because he borrowed your CD player and broke it. What can you do to help you deal with your anger?

You are upset because your parents said they would take you swimming, but they changed their minds because they were too tired. What can you do to help you deal with your feelings?

Name an adult you admire who appropriately deals with frustration or anger. Explain how he/she deals with anger.

You are mad at someone in your class because he made fun of you in front of everyone. What can you do to deal with your anger?

Explain how you feel mentally when you are angry. What thoughts do you have? What messages do you tell yourself? What things do you care about?

You are upset because someone keeps telling your friends not to hang out with you. What can you do to deal with your anger?

You are mad because a boy in your class talked about your mom. What can you do to help you with your anger?

Super Prizes

Sorry, just 5 points.

For 25 points, bark like a dog.

For 20 points, hold your nose and say your full name 10 times.

You get to keep your 10 points.

Hooray – you get 30 points.

Sorry, just 5 points.

You get to keep your 10 points.

For 25 points, do a hula dance.

For 20 points, do the bunny hop around your desk

Hooray – you get 30 points.

For 20 points, try to pronounce your name spelled backwards.

For 25 points, skip to the front of the room and back.

You get to keep your 10 points.

For 20 points, spin around in a circle five times.

Hooray – you get 30 points.

Sorry, just 5 points.

For 25 points, jump up and down 15 times.

You get to keep your 10 points.

Super Prizes

Sorry, just 5 points.	For 20 points, you must try to say the alphabet backwards.	For 25 points, you must do 20 jumping jacks.
You get to keep your 10 points.	Hooray – you get 30 points.	Sorry, just 5 points.
You get to keep your 10 points.	For 20 points, you must do the twist for one minute.	For 25 points, try to balance your pencil on the end of your finger.
Hooray – you get 30 points.	For 20 points, walk 10 steps with a book on your head.	Sorry, just 5 points.
You get to keep your 10 points.	You get to keep your 10 points.	Hooray – you get 30 points.
Sorry, just 5 points.	Hooray – you get 30 points.	You get to keep your 10 points.

Dear Parents/Guardians,

Today, your child participated in a classroom guidance game entitled, "Super Prize." The objective of this game was to teach students the importance of anger control at school and at home. We talked about ways to vent anger and to avoid blowing up at people such as playing outside, playing a game, having some time by yourself, talking with somebody, writing in a journal, listening to music, drawing, or watching a show.

In our game, students were divided into two teams. Teams competed for points by answering questions about ways to control anger. After correctly answering questions, players could risk giving up their points for one of the "super prizes" found in three different envelopes. By taking this risk, players could lose points, gain extra points, or earn points by engaging in silly behaviors such as doing the twist.

At home tonight, you can talk to your child about how everyone gets angry and that it is okay to be angry. You can encourage your child to continue to deal with anger in appropriate ways.

Thanks for your support,

Square Feelings

Grade Levels
2-6

Materials
- Markers
- 2 Large Sheets of Paper

Time Needed
Approximately 30 minutes

Skills Covered
- Understanding & Communicating Feelings of Self and Others

Introduction
Teams compete against one another by correctly defining feelings that belong in different situations and connecting two dots on the "Make A Square" paper. Each time a team connects the last two dots of a square, that team gets one point. The team with the most completed squares wins the game.

Pre-Game Directions
1. On one large sheet of butcher paper, write "MAKE A SQUARE" in large letters across the top.

2. Below the "MAKE A SQUARE" title, draw 36 dots, 6 rows across and 6 rows down.

3. Hang the "Make a Square" paper in front of the classroom.

4. On another large sheet of paper, write, "FEELINGS WORD BANK."

Game Directions
1. Divide class into two teams.

2. Player from Team A writes down one feeling word in the Feelings Word Bank and then connects two dots on the Make a Square Page.

3. Each time a team connects the last two dots that complete a square, that team writes the letter for their team (A or B) inside the completed square and receives a point.

4. After each player has added a word to the Feelings Word Bank, next player, and all players thereafter, must use a word from the Feelings Word Bank to describe an actual or fictional situation in which a person felt this feeling. If the word is used correctly, player can connect two dots on the Make a Square Page.

5. Play as time allows. Team with the most points wins the game.

Follow-Up
- Do you think it is easier for adults or kids to talk about their feelings? Explain why.
- What was your favorite emotion word discussed today? Explain why.
- Write a short paper entitled, "A Day that I Felt _____." Fill in the blank with one of the words used in today's game.

Dear Parents/Guardians,

Today, your child participated in a classroom guidance game entitled, "Square Feelings." The objective of this game was to help students improve their understanding of their own feelings, as well as the feelings of others.

In this game, the class was divided into two teams. Teams competed to complete a square on a dot matrix. Players first created a word bank of feelings. For each word contributed to the bank, players connected two dots on the matrix. After creating the word bank, each player had to use a word from the bank to describe an actual or fictional situation in which a person felt this feeling in order to connect two dots. Each time a square was completed on the matrix, the team that connected the last line of the square received one point.

At home tonight, you can talk to your child about adults with whom your child is comfortable talking about his/her feelings. You can encourage your child to talk to others about things that bother or concern him/her.

Thanks for your support,

Emotion-Behavior Act-Out

Grade Levels
2-6

Materials
- Copy of Emotion-Behavior Act-Out Cards (pp.196-197)
- Piece of Poster Board or Butcher Paper
- Magic Marker

Time Needed
Approximately 30 minutes

Skills Covered
- Conflict Resolution
- Getting Along With Others

Introduction
This game is similar to Charades. Teams compete against one another to guess the actions as well as the feelings in each Act-Out.

Pre-Game Directions

1. Explain to class that they will be participating in a game where they will have the opportunity to silently act out scenarios for their teams and their teams can guess the behavior and the emotion.

2. Talk about the importance of understanding the feelings of others. Say to the class something like, "If one of your friends comes to school and is crying – should you start talking to her about the new movie you want to see this weekend?" Ask the class about how they would know she was upset and what they could do to help her feel better.

3. Go over the ten emotions - sad, mad, frustrated, disappointed, scared, happy, excited, surprised, pleased and relaxed - that will be used in this game. Write them down on the piece of butcher paper for the students. Hang paper in front of room.

Game Directions

1. Divide class into two teams.

2. Two players from Team A will pick an Emotion-Behavior Act-Out Card.

3. The players will silently act out the situation described on the cards to their team.

4. The teams have two minutes to guess the behaviors and the emotions described on the cards.

5. The teams gets one point for correctly guessing the behaviors and one point for correctly guessing the emotions.

4. Repeat steps #2-5 for Team B.

5. Proceed with game as time allows. The team with the most points wins the game.

Game Variation

- Players must describe an appropriate follow-up or solution to each situation described on the cards.

Emotion-Behavior Act-Out Cards

SAD
You are sad because your friend has been teasing you.

SAD
You are sad because your friend has not been talking to you.

SAD
You are sad because your dog died.

MAD

You are mad because you and your friend had an argument.

MAD

You are mad because no one will let you play basketball.

MAD
You are mad because your mom punished you.

SURPRISED
You are surprised because you won an award for being a great soccer player.

SURPRISED
You are surprised because your dad took you to get ice cream.

SURPRISED
You are surprised because you got a present from your aunt in the mail.

PLEASED

You are pleased because you learned all your spelling words.

PLEASED

You are pleased because you found a book you thought you lost.

PLEASED

You are pleased because your team won the basketball game.

RELAXED
You are relaxed because you are watching television.

RELAXED
You are relaxed because you are playing your game.

RELAXED
You are relaxed because you are reading a book.

Emotion-Behavior Act-Out Cards

FRUSTRATED
You are frustrated because you failed your test.

FRUSTRATED
You are frustrated because you do not understand your math homework.

FRUSTRATED
You are frustrated because you are having trouble hitting the ball in baseball.

SCARED

You are scared because you woke up and could not find your parents.

SCARED

You are scared to spend the night away from home.

SCARED
You are scared because someone said that he is gong to get you after school.

EXCITED
You are excited because you did a great job on your report card.

EXCITED
You are excited because it is your birthday.

EXCITED
You are excited because you are going to a party.

HAPPY

You are happy because you are hanging out with your friends.

HAPPY

You are happy because you got some money for your birthday.

HAPPY

You are happy because you got an A on a test.

DISAPPOINTED
You are disappointed because you failed a test.

DISAPPOINTED
You are disappointed because you did not score during your basketball game.

DISAPPOINTED
You are disappointed because you struck out in your baseball game.

Dear Parents/Guardians,

Today, your child participated in a classroom guidance game entitled, "Emotion-Behavior Act-Out." The objective of this game was to teach students ways to appropriately respond to the emotions of others. We talked about ways to know how others are feeling and ways to help others feel better.

In this game, the class was divided into two teams. Players picked cards with scenarios portraying different emotions. Players acted out the scenarios for their teams. Teams had to correctly guess the emotions, as well as the behaviors in order to receive two points.

At home tonight, you can talk to your child about appropriate ways to respond to different situations such as a friend that is crying or a brother that is frustrated with math. You can encourage your child to talk about actual situations where he/she has responded to the emotions of others.

Thanks for your support,

Uncover It!

Game #39

Grade Levels
2-6

Materials
- Copy of Uncover It! Words (pg.200)
- Chalkboard, Whiteboard, or Large Sheets of Paper

Time Needed
Approximately 30 minutes

Skills Covered
- Understanding & Communicating Feelings of Self and Others

Introduction

This is a great classroom game that concentrates on spelling, defining, and understanding emotions!

Pre-Game Directions

1. Explain to class that they will be participating in a classroom game where they will be competing to uncover words that describe emotions.

2. Tell the class that they will be divided into four teams. Teams will get points for correctly guessing letters and even more points for correctly guessing the word.

Game Directions

1. Divide the class into four teams. Allow the teams to make up names for themselves.

2. Draw blanks on the board, one for each letter in the word. For example, the word "ANGRY" would have five blanks.

3. Player from Team A may guess any letter. If the letter is part of the word, complete the blank(s) where the letter(s) belong.

4. If the player correctly guesses a letter, the team gets 10 points for each blank that letter fills. For example, if the word is "HAPPY" and the person guesses "P", the team would get 10 points for each P – resulting in 20 points for that team.

5. The next teams repeat steps 4 and 5.

6. At any time, a team may attempt to guess the word. If they correctly guess the word, the team will be awarded 40 points. The team will be awarded an extra 20 points if the team player can correctly use the word in a sentence.

7. If a team player incorrectly guesses a word, 50 points will be deducted from that team's points.

8. Record the points for each team on the board.

9. Once the word has been correctly guessed, begin the game again with another word.

10. Play as time allows. Team with the most points wins the game.

Game Variation

- Play game as described above. In addition, players must describe a time that they felt the uncovered word for an extra 20 points.

Uncover It! Words

Peaceful

Angry

Disappointed

Thrilled

Scared

Calm

Upset

Happy

Worried

Relaxed

Tired

Pleased

Excited

Dear Parents/Guardians,

Today, your child participated in a classroom guidance game entitled, "Uncover It." The objective of this game was to help students increase their knowledge and understanding of different emotions.

In this game, students were divided into two teams. Teams competed to fill in the blanks to discover the different emotions such as joyful, peaceful, angry, disappointed, scared, thrilled, calm, upset, worried, happy, relaxed, tired, pleased, and excited. Teams received points for correctly guessed letters, for correctly guessing the emotion, and for correctly using the word in a sentence.

At home tonight, you can play your own game of "Uncover It" with your family!

Thanks for your support,

Game #40

Grade Levels

2-6

Materials

- Copy of Emotional Hodgepodge Cards (pp.204-205)
- Modeling Clay for Each Team
- Large Pieces of Paper or Whiteboard for Each Team
- Crayons or Markers for Each Team
- Small Table for Each Team

Time Needed

Approximately 30 minutes

Skills Covered

- Understanding & Communicating Feelings of Self and Others

Emotional Hodgepodge

Introduction

This is a great game that focuses on emotions. Students love this game because it has something for everyone – modeling with clay, acting out, and drawing pictures.

Pre-Game Directions

1. Copy and cut out Emotional Hodgepodge Cards.

2. Place clay, paper, and markers on a table for each team's use.

3. Explain to class that they will be participating in a game that requires a variety of talents – acting out, drawing, spelling, describing, and modeling with clay. Along with these talents, the game also requires identifying emotions.

4. Talk to students about the importance of understanding the feelings of others. Ask students what they should do if someone is sitting by him/herself during recess. Ask students how they think that person feels. Ask students to provide other examples of ways they can help other students with hurt, sad, or angry feelings.

5. Explain that during this game, the class will be divided into teams of 3-5 students. Teams will compete against each other for points by acting out, modeling with clay, drawing, filling in blanks to spell an emotion, or defining an emotion. Teams have one minute to guess the emotions.

6. Write down the following emotion words on a large piece of paper: happy, tired, sad, worried, excited, relaxed, mad, disappointed, elated, angry, frustrated, surprised, joyful, peaceful, thrilled, and scared.

7. Review the emotion words with the class – make sure they understand the meaning of the words. Remove the paper containing the emotion words before beginning the game.

8. Explain that the teams will take turns. A member from the team will pick an Emotional Hodgepodge Card. According to the card, the team member will need to silently model with clay, silently draw pictures depicting the emotion, complete blanks in order to spell an emotion, describe an emotion, or act out an emotion. If the team correctly guesses the emotion, the team will receive five points.

Emotional Hodgepodge

Game Directions

1. Divide the class into teams of 3-5 students.

2. Allow each team to give themselves a team name.

3. One player from Team A gets to choose an Emotional Hodgepodge Card.

4. The player must follow the directions on the card and their team must try to guess the emotion described on the card.

5. Five points will be awarded for correctly guessed emotions.

6. Remaining teams proceed as Team A.

7. Game continues as time allows. Team with most points wins the game.

Follow-Up

- Which activity did you enjoy the most in the game – modeling with clay, drawing pictures, spelling the word, describing the word, or acting out the word? Explain why.
- Do you think that any of these activities (drawing, playing with clay, talking or moving around) are techniques that you can use to deal with anxiety or to let go of your feelings?
- Do you think that any of these activities can help you in dealing with your own emotions and communicating your feelings to others?

Materials

- Copy of Emotional Hodgepodge Cards (pp.204-205)
- Modeling Clay for Each Team
- Large Pieces of Paper or Whiteboard for Each Team
- Crayons or Markers for Each Team
- Small Table for Each Team

Time Needed

Approximately 30 minutes

Skills Covered

- Understanding & Communicating Feelings of Self and Others

Emotional Hodgepodge Cards

Write the following on a sheet of paper for your team. Your team must correctly fill in the blanks to guess this emotion.

__e__a__ed

Answer: RELAXED

Silently act out the following emotion for your team:

SAD

Silently draw pictures and have your team guess the following emotion:

FURIOUS

With clay or dough, try to model the following emotion and your team must guess it:

HAPPY

Describe the following emotion to your team:

WORRIED

Write the following on a sheet of paper for your team. Your team must correctly fill in the blanks to guess this emotion:

__i__ed

Answer: TIRED

Silently act out the following emotion for your team:

EXCITED

Silently draw pictures and have your team guess the following emotion:

DISAPPOINTED

Write the following on a sheet of paper for your team. Your team must correctly fill in the blanks to guess this emotion.

__L__T__D

Answer: ELATED

With clay or dough, try to model the following emotion and your team must guess it:

MAD

Describe the following emotion to your team:

SURPRISED

Silently act out the following emotion for your team:

JOYFUL

Silently draw pictures and have your team guess the following emotion:

SCARED

With clay or dough, try to model the following emotion and your team must guess it:

ANGRY

Describe the following emotion to your team:

PEACEFUL

Emotional Hodgepodge Cards

Write the following on a sheet of paper for your team. Your team must correctly fill in the blanks to guess this emotion.

_ _ R _ RIS _ D
Answer: SURPRISED

Silently act out the following emotion for your team:

FRUSTRATED

Silently draw pictures and have your team guess the following emotion:

JOYFUL

With clay or dough, try to model the following emotion and your team must guess it:

TIRED

Describe the following emotion to your team:

WORRIED

Write the following on a sheet of paper for your team. Your team must correctly fill in the blanks to guess this emotion:

_ _ ri _ _ ed
Answer: THRILLED

Silently act out the following emotion for your team:

DISAPPOINTED

Silently draw pictures and have your team guess the following emotion:

SAD

With clay or dough, try to model the following emotion and your team must guess it:

THRILLED

Describe the following emotion to your team:

WORRIED

Write the following on a sheet of paper for your team. Your team must correctly fill in the blanks to guess this emotion.

_ X _ I _ ED
Answer: Excited

Silently act out the following emotion for your team:

TIRED

Silently draw pictures and have your team guess the following emotion:

ELATED

With clay or dough, try to model the following emotion and your team must guess it:

SCARED

Describe the following emotion to your team:

JOYFUL

Dear Parents/Guardians,

Today, your child participated in a classroom guidance game entitled, "Emotional Hodgepodge." The objective of this game was to help students learn and practice ways to understand feelings, communicate feelings, and help others with their feelings. We talked about the importance of reaching out to others.

In this game, students were divided into teams of 3-5 students. Teams competed against each other for points by drawing emotions, describing emotions, acting out emotions, spelling emotions, and even modeling emotions out of clay!

At home tonight, you can talk to your child about reasons why people have difficulty talking about their feelings. You can ask your child to identify some emotions that he/she has difficulty discussing. You can encourage your child to talk to you or another adult, even when it is difficult to do so.

Thanks for your support,

Classmate Match

Game #41

Grade Levels
2-6

Materials
- Copy of Classmate Match Board for Each Student (pg.209)
- Pencil For Each Student

Time Needed
Approximately 30 minutes

Skills Covered
- Self-Esteem
- Positive Communication

Introduction

This game gets students moving around and getting to know everyone in their class. It can help break down cliques by encouraging students to talk to everyone.

Pre-Game Directions

1. Explain to the class that they will be participating in a game where they will get to learn new and interesting things about their classmates.

2. Talk about how everyone has individual and unique characteristics. Ask the students what their class, their school, their family, and their world would be like if everyone liked the same things and was talented in the same areas. This would mean that we would only have one kind of music, a few types of food, a few types of clothes – and everyone would look and act the same. Talk about how boring this would make our school and our world.

3. Talk about the importance of respecting and appreciating our differences. We should make sure that we get to know everyone and learn about the likes, dislikes, talents and interests of our fellow classmates.

4. Explain to the class that they will each be getting a Classmate Match Board. They must find one person in their class that fits the description in each box. That person must sign his/her name to the box. The same person can only sign two boxes. The first person to have a student signature in every box will win the game.

Game Directions
Part One

1. Give each student a Classmate Match Board.

2. Tell the students to begin finding students to sign the boxes on their boards. Remind students that one student may only sign one or two boxes – they may not sign more than two.

3. The first person to have a board with signatures in every box wins that game.

Game #41

Grade Levels

2-6

Materials

- Copy of Classmate Match Board for Each Student (pg.209)
- Pencil For Each Student

Time Needed

Approximately 30 minutes

Skills Covered

- Self-Esteem
- Positive Communication

Classmate Match

Game Directions
Part Two

1. Instruct students to stand in front of their desks.

2. Read the title from the first box – Has Musical Talent. Instruct all students that have musical talents to go to the right side of the classroom. Ask students to return to their desks.

3. Read title from the next box – Plays Football. Instruct all students that play football to come to the front of the classroom. Ask students to return to their desks.

4. Continue reading titles from the boxes on the Classmate Match Board and instructing students who meet this criteria to move to a different part of the classroom.

Follow-Up

- What did you learn about your classmates?
- What things did you learn about your class as a whole? Discuss the uniqueness of your class.
- Which of the boxes on the Classmate Match Board did you like talking about the most? Why?
- Do you think it is hard to get to know people at school? Explain why.

Classmate Match Board

Has Musical Talent	Plays Football	Collects Something	Was Born in a Different State
Has Gone to This School Since Kindergarten	Moved to This School This Year	Loves the Color Purple	Can Curl His/Her Tongue
Can Whistle	Can Do Twenty Push-Ups	Loves to Run	Has Traveled Outside of the USA
Has No Brothers or Sisters	Loves to Dance	Loves to Read	Is Wearing Something Red
Middle Name Has More Than 7 Letters	Is Wearing Shoes With No Shoelaces	Likes to Shop	Loves Math
Can Do a Flip	Has Painted Toenails	Has More Than 4 Pets	Has Long Hair

Dear Parents/Guardians,

Today, your child participated in a classroom guidance game entitled, "Classmate Match." The objective of this game was to help students reach out to others and learn about the likes, dislikes, talents and interests of their classmates. We discussed the importance of respecting and appreciating our differences.

In this game, each student was given a Classmate Match Board with boxes describing interesting, unique characteristics. Students raced to complete their Classmate Match Boards by finding classmates who fit the descriptions in each box on the boards. Afterwards, the class discussed the characteristics on the boards and students were able to share their own unique traits.

At home tonight, you can ask your child about things he/she learned about his/her classmates. You can talk to your child about the importance of being proud of his/her unique traits.

Thanks for your support,

Anger Control Beanbag Toss

Introduction

This game is a great way for students to learn ways to control their anger while playing a game of beanbag toss.

Pre-Game Directions

1. Copy and cut out Anger Control Cards.

2. Cut out the inside of each of the coffee can lids to make rings.

3. Number each ring - #1, #2, #3, or #4.

4. Place the piece of paper in the front of the classroom to specify a student marker where the students will stand when tossing the beanbags.

5. Strategically place the four rings in a vertical line in front of the student marker. Ring #1 should be closest to the marker where the students will stand. Ring #4 should be the furthest away from the student marker.

6. Hang piece of butcher paper in front of room.

7. Explain to class that they will be participating in a game of Anger Control Beanbag Toss.

8. Talk to the students about the difficulties of controlling their anger in different situations. Say to the class, "If someone makes fun of you, how does it make you feel and what does it make you want to do?" Talk about how this situation and the different reactions the students might have. Talk about why it is important to react appropriately, rather than inappropriately (hitting, pushing, saying inappropriate things).

9. Encourage the class to brainstorm different appropriate reactions to angry situations. Write these down on the large sheet of paper in front of the classroom. Label this paper, "Appropriate Ways to Handle Anger."

10. Explain to the class that they will be divided into two teams. The teams will be competing against one another by answering anger control questions for five points and tossing the beanbags for additional points.

Grade

2-6

Materials

- 4 Beanbags
- 4 Coffee Can Lids
- Scissors
- Copy of Anger Control Cards (pp.213-214)
- Piece of Paper / Other Marker
- Magic Markers
- Large Sheet of Paper

Time Needed

Approximately 30 minutes

Skills Covered

- Anger Control
- Positive Communication
- Conflict Resolution

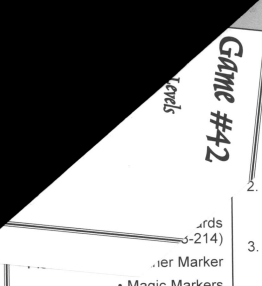

Levels

...rds
...5-214)

...ier Marker
• Magic Markers
• Large Sheet of Paper

Time Needed

Approximately 30 minutes

Skills Covered

• Anger Control
• Positive Communication
• Conflict Resolution

Anger Control Beanbag Toss

Directions

1. Divide class into two teams.

2. Player from Team A chooses an Anger Control Card. Player answers question. Encourage students to use the "Appropriate Ways to Handle Anger" for assistance in thinking of answers.

3. If answered correctly, Team A receives five points and player has opportunity to get more points by tossing the beanbags. Player stands on student marker and gently tosses each of the four beanbags. If any beanbags land inside a ring, Team A receives the number of points for which that ring is marked. For example, if the beanbags land in Ring #1 and Ring #4, Team A receives an additional 5 points (1 for Ring #1 and 4 for Ring #4).

4. Team B proceeds as Team A.

5. Game continues as time allows. The team with the most points wins the game.

Follow-Up

• Which one of the examples in today's game would anger you the most if it happened to you? Explain why. Describe an appropriate reaction.
• If people know different ways to appropriately respond to a situation that makes them angry, why do they still react inappropriately at times? What do you think could help them to react in an appropriate way?
• Do you think adults understand the things that make kids angry? Explain your answer.
• Do you think kids understand the things that make adults angry? Explain your answer.

Anger Control Cards

What is an appropriate way to react if someone knocks you and your books down?

What is an appropriate way to react if your mom punishes you and takes your game away?

What is an appropriate way to react if you were blamed for something that you did not do?

What is an appropriate way to react if you were punished for acting up in class, but nobody else was punished?

What is an appropriate way to react if your friends laugh and whisper to each other every time you stand near them?

What is an appropriate way to react if your friends are not hanging out with you at recess?

What is an appropriate way to react if someone rolls his eyes at you when your teacher turns around?

What is an appropriate way to react if someone keeps picking on your little sister?

What is an appropriate way to react if someone tells other people to not be your friend?

What is an appropriate way to react if someone says that you cannot play baseball with him because you are not good at baseball?

What is an appropriate way to react if someone says that your mom cannot afford to buy you new clothes?

What is an appropriate way to react if your teacher punishes you for talking and you were not talking?

What is an appropriate way to react if someone takes your pencil?

What is an appropriate way to react if someone makes fun of the way you run?

What is an appropriate way to react if one of your friends says that you cannot come to a party at his house?

Anger Control Cards

What is an appropriate way to react if you want to go over to your friend's house and your mom will not let you?

What is an appropriate way to react if you want to stay up late and watch a movie and your dad says you have to go to bed?

What is an appropriate way to react if you forgot to study for your test and you get a bad grade on it?

What is an appropriate way to react if your teacher does not let you go to recess because you did not do your homework?

What is an appropriate way to react if you cannot understand the new math concepts your teacher is teaching you?

What is an appropriate way to react if someone makes fun of the way you dance?

What is an appropriate way to react if someone says that she does not want to be your friend anymore?

What is an appropriate way to react if someone says that he is better in football than you?

What is an appropriate way to react if someone says that she has better clothes than you?

What is an appropriate way to react if someone cuts in front of you in the lunch line?

What is an appropriate way to react if someone says that you live in an ugly house?

What is an appropriate way to react if someone makes fun of your mom's car?

What is an appropriate way to react if someone says that no one wants you to hang out with them anymore?

What is an appropriate way to react if someone calls you stupid?

What is an appropriate way to react if someone says that your hair looks gross?

Dear Parents/Guardians,

Today, your child participated in a classroom guidance game entitled, "Anger Control Beanbag Toss." The objective of this game was to teach students appropriate ways to express their anger and ways to control their anger. As a class, we brainstormed ways to appropriately handle anger. We talked about why we should control our anger.

In this game, students were divided into two teams. Players picked question cards that described possible angry situations. In order to earn points, players had to state appropriate reactions. Teams earned additional points by tossing four beanbags into small rings.

At home tonight, you can talk with your child about why people respond inappropriately if they know appropriate responses to angry situations. You can talk to your child about things that adults can do to help kids act appropriately when they are angry.

Thanks for your support,

Chapter Six

Responsibility

Games in this chapter concentrate on goal setting, study skills, and career information for grades 2-6.

Career Charades

Introduction

A great game for everyone! It requires little to no preparation, it helps students explore and learn about careers, and students are able to interact, be creative, and move around!

Pre-Game Directions

1. Copy and cut out Career Charades Cards.

2. Hang sheet of paper in front of room. Label this paper, "Careers."

3. Explain to the class that they will be exploring and learning about many different careers.

4. Ask the class to think of careers they have seen or heard about and write them down on the "Careers" paper. Make sure that all careers listed on the Career Charades Cards are included on the "Careers" paper.

5. Briefly discuss each of the careers on the "Careers" paper, including job duties and where these jobs take place. Before beginning the game, remove the paper.

6. Explain to the class that they will be divided into two teams and will be competing against each other in a game of charades where they will silently act out different careers.

Game Directions

1. Two players from Team A choose a Career Charades Card.

2. Team A players have less than two minutes to look at the card and think about how one of them will silently act out the career to their team.

3. One of the Team A players will have two minutes to silently act out the career for Team A. If team correctly guesses the career within two minutes, Team A gets one point.

4. Team B proceeds as Team A.

5. Continue as time allows. Team with the most points wins.

Grade Levels

2-6

Materials

- Copy of Career Charades Cards (pp.219-220)
- Large Sheet of Paper
- Markers

Time Needed

Approximately 30 minutes

Skills Covered

- Career Information and Exploration
- Goal Setting

Game #43

Grade Levels

2-6

Materials

• Copy of Career Charades Cards (pp.219-220)

• Large Sheet of Paper

• Markers

Time Needed

Approximately 30 minutes

Skills Covered

• Career Information and Exploration

• Goal Setting

Career Charades

Follow-Up

• Pick one career that you would like to learn more about. What are some questions that you have about this career?

• Help the class make career vests. Use brown paper bags and cut off the bottoms. Cut a vertical line down the middle of the bag (from top to bottom). Cut two armholes. Decorate the vest like the career in which you are interested. For example, if your career of interest were a police officer, you might color the vest blue and draw a badge, whistle, holster, etc.

• Write a short paragraph about the career you chose. Wear your vest and read your paragraph to the class.

Career Charades Cards

TEACHER

WAITER / WAITRESS

NURSE

CHEF

COACH

SECRETARY

FIRE FIGHTER

POLICE OFFICER

CASHIER

DENTIST
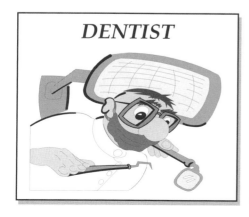

DOCTOR

FLORIST

Career Charades Cards

MECHANIC

HAIRDRESSER

CARPENTER

COMPUTER TECHNICIAN

PILOT

VETERINARIAN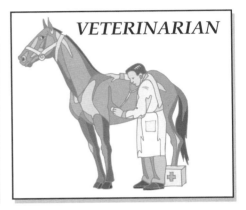

REALTOR

PRINCIPAL

ELECTRICIAN

PASTOR

ARTIST

ACTRESS **ACTOR**

Dear Parents/Guardians,

Today, your child participated in a classroom guidance game entitled, "Career Charades." The objective of this game was to help students learn about and explore different careers. As a class, we brainstormed many different careers. We talked about each of these jobs, including where these jobs take place and a brief description of job duties.

In this game, the class was divided into two teams. Players picked cards with the names of different careers on them. Teams competed for points by acting out the chosen careers for their teams. Teams earned points by correctly guessing the careers.

At home tonight, you can talk to your child about the different careers he/she learned about in our game. You can talk to your child about your career or the careers of family members.

Thanks for your support,

Game #44

Copyright YouthLight, Inc.

Grade Levels

2-6

Materials

- Copy of Career Hush Cards (pp.224-225)
- Large Sheet of Butcher Paper
- Magic Marker

Time Needed

Approximately 30 minutes

Skills Covered

- Career Information and Exploration
- Goal Setting

Career Hush

Introduction

A fun game that helps students learn about and explore careers.

Pre-Game Directions

1. Copy and cut out Career Hush Cards.

2. Hang paper in front of classroom.

3. Write down the following thirty careers on the large sheet of paper: teacher, secretary, dentist, doctor, teacher, principal, counselor, carpenter, mechanic, plumber, electrician, coach, veterinarian, artist, florist, librarian, realtor, actor/actress, pilot, orthodontist, computer technician, construction worker, cashier, waiter/waitress, nurse, chef, secretary, coach, nurse, firefighter, and painter. Before beginning the game, remove this paper.

4. Encourage the students to think of descriptive words for each of the thirty careers.

5. Explain to the class that they will be participating in a game where they will need to try to describe careers to each other WITHOUT using certain key "hush" words. Give the class an example such as describing a teacher without using the words "teach" or "school." Explain to the class that they could describe a teacher as someone who works with children and helps them learn.

Game Directions

1. Divide class into two teams.

2. Player from Team A picks a Career Hush Card. Player A has one minute to think about ways to describe the career to his/her team.

3. Player A has two minutes to describe the career to his/her team. If the team correctly guesses the career within two minutes and the player does not use any of the hush words, the team will get five points.

4. If Player A accidentally uses any of the "hush words" written on the card, and the team correctly guesses the career within two minutes, the team will only be able to receive two points.

5. Team B proceeds as Team A.

6. Continue as time allows. Team with the most points wins.

Career Hush

Follow-Up

- Have the class create their own Career Hush Cards. Assign each student a career. Help the students research these careers and write down short descriptions of these careers.
- Give each student an index card. Instruct the students to write down the career they researched at the top of the card. Tell the students to write down two words that describe this career underneath the name of the career. These two words will be the "hush" words for the card.
- Play the game of Career Hush using the cards created by the class.

Game #44

Grade Levels

2-6

Materials

- Copy of Career Hush Cards (pp.224-225)
- Large Sheet of Butcher Paper
- Magic Marker

Time Needed

Approximately 30 minutes

Skills Covered

- Career Information and Exploration
- Goal Setting

Career Hush Cards

TEACHER

Hush words:

Students

School

SECRETARY

Hush words:

Phone

Desk

DENTIST

Hush words:

Teeth

Mouth

DOCTOR

Hush words:

Shots

Sick

PRINCIPAL

Hush words:

School

Trouble

COUNSELOR

Hush words:

Problems

Talk

CARPENTER

Hush words:

Build

Wood

MECHANIC

Hush words:

Fix

Cars

PLUMBER

Hush words:

Fix

Pipes

ELECTRICIAN

Hush words:

Electricity

Fix

COACH

Hush words:

Sports

Games

VETERINARIAN

Hush words:

Animals

Doctor

ARTIST

Hush words:

Paints

Draws

FLORIST

Hush words:

Arrange

Flowers

LIBRARIAN

Hush words:

Books

School

Career Hush Cards

MUSICIAN
Hush words:

Music

Sings

ACTOR / ACTRESS
Hush words:

Television

Movies

PILOT
Hush words:

Airplane

Flies

ORTHODONTIST
Hush words:

Braces

Teeth

COMPUTER TECHNICIAN
Hush words:

Computers

Fixes

CONSTRUCTION WORKER
Hush words:

Builds

Houses

CASHIER
Hush words:

Cash Register

Store

WAITER / WAITRESS
Hush words:

Restaurant

Food

CHEF
Hush words:

Cooks

Food

REALTOR
Hush words:

Houses

Sell

COACH
Hush words:

Students

Sports

NURSE
Hush words:

Doctor

Shots

FIRE FIGHTER
Hush words:

Fire

Hose

PAINTER
Hush words:

Paint

Houses

POLICE OFFICER
Hush words:

Uniform

Cop

Dear Parents/Guardians,

Today, your child participated in a classroom guidance game entitled, "Career Hush." The objective of this game was to learn and practice knowledge of different careers. We discussed many different careers such as: teacher, secretary, dentist, doctor, teacher, principal, counselor, carpenter, mechanic, plumber, electrician, coach, veterinarian, artist, florist, librarian, realtor, actor/actress, pilot, orthodontist, computer technician, construction worker, cashier, waiter/waitress, nurse, chef, secretary, coach, nurse, firefighter, and painter.

In this game, the class was divided into two teams. Players picked cards with the names of careers on them. Players described these careers to their teams, but could not use certain "hush" words in their explanations. For example, for "teacher," players could not use the words "students" or "school." Teams earned points by correctly guessing the careers.

At home tonight, you can talk to your child about the different careers discussed in our game.

Thanks for your support,

Responsible Soccer Game

Game #45

Grade Levels
2-6

Materials
- Copy of Soccer Field (pg.229)
- Copy of Study Skills Soccer Cards (pp.231-232)
- Soccer Ball / Other Ball
- Tape
- Copy of Soccer Goal (pg.230)

Time Needed
Approximately 30 minutes

Skills Covered
- Responsible Behaviors
- Goal Setting
- Achieving Goals

Introduction
This game is a great indoor game of soccer while practicing responsibility.

Pre-Game Directions
1. Cut out the two soccer balls. Place a piece of tape on the back of each paper soccer ball.
2. Cut out and tape copy of soccer field on board.
3. Tape copy of soccer goal on bottom of wall or classroom door.
4. Talk to the students about the importance of responsibility. Ask students about the different areas in which they should be responsible – goal setting, study skills, ownership of actions, etc.
5. Explain that you will be playing a game of soccer where you will answer questions about ways to behave responsibly.

Game Directions
1. Divide class into two teams –Lightning Bolts and Shining Stars.
2. Tape the Lightning Bolt soccer ball on the lightning bolt player marked "1." Tape the Shining Star soccer ball on the shining star player marked "1."
3. The first student from the Lightning Bolt Team draws a card. If the student answers the responsible question correctly, the team can move their soccer ball the number of passes marked on the card. For example, if the card states "3 passes", the soccer ball is moved from player #1 to player #4.
4. The Shining Stars team proceeds in same manner as the Lightning Bolt team.
5. The first team to reach the goal gets one point. The team gets the opportunity to get an extra point by having one student kick the soccer ball and hit the paper soccer goal taped on wall.
6. Both teams return the paper soccer balls to player #1. The team that did not get the last goal gets to go first. Game continues to proceed as described in #3.
7. At the end of the time allotted for the game, the team with the most points wins.

Game #45

2-6

Materials

- Copy of Soccer Field (pg.229)
- Copy of Study Skills Soccer Cards (pp.231-232)
- Soccer Ball / Other Ball
- Tape
- Copy of Soccer Goal (pg.230)

Time Needed

Approximately 30 minutes

Skills Covered

- Responsible Behaviors
- Goal Setting
- Achieving Goals

Responsible Soccer Game

Follow-Up

- What are some things that are difficult to plan? Do you have more or less trouble planning and beginning activities that you do not like to do?
- Use your dictionary to define the word "procrastinate." Why do you think people procrastinate? Do you ever procrastinate? If so, what activities do you procrastinate?
- Why is it important to finish an activity once you start it or give a commitment? For example, if you sign up for baseball, why is it important to go to all the practices and games? What would happen if people quit activities whenever they felt like it?

Responsible Soccer

✂ Cut along
dotted lines.

Responsible Soccer

Responsible Soccer Game Cards

Today is Tuesday. You have a project due on Friday. Explain what you should do on Tuesday, Wednesday, and Thursday to get ready for your project.

3 Passes

Your mom asked you to clean your room. Your neighbor asked you to play football. What should you do?

2 Passes

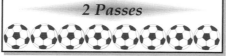

Your teacher asked you to read over your notes from class today for homework. You are really tired. What should you do?

1 Pass

Your dad asked you to pick up sticks in your yard. Your favorite show is on television. What should you do?

3 Passes

You would like to play football in the fall. What are some things you can do to help prepare for football?

2 Passes

Your friend asked you to come over. Later someone else asked you to go skating. You really want to go skating, but you first said you would go to your friend's house. What should you do?

1 Pass

Name five study skills that you need to use when taking a test.

3 Passes

Name three things that a well-prepared student should have in his backpack.

2 Passes

Describe how a well-prepared student's desk should look.

1 Pass

You are almost finished with your homework and a show is on that you really want to watch. Your mom asks if you finished your homework. What should you do?

3 Passes

Your dad asked you to watch your little brother. You want to check on a show really quickly that is on in another room that your little brother is not allowed in. What should you do?

2 Passes

Your mom asked you to clean out your backpack before you go outside. You really want to go outside and you do not want to clean everything out of your backpack. What should you do?

1 Pass

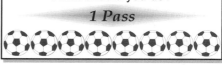

You told your friend that you would sit beside her on the bus. However, in the afternoon, someone else asks you to sit beside her. What should you do?

3 Passes

You know that you cannot talk on the phone until your chores are done. You are almost finished with your chores when your friend calls. What should you do?

2 Passes

You told your dad that if he let you skip cleaning your room yesterday, you would clean it today. However, today you want to go over to your neighbor's house. What should you do?

1 Pass

Responsible Soccer Game Cards

Name three things a responsible student does when the teacher is talking.

3 Passes

Name three things you need to do to improve your responsible behaviors.

2 Passes

Name three responsible behaviors that you are great at doing.

1 Pass

You have a test on Thursday. Today is Monday. What should do Monday, Tuesday, and Wednesday to get ready for your test?

3 Passes

You promised your friend you would play basketball during recess. When recess starts, some other people ask you to play baseball. What should you do?

2 Passes

You told your mom that if she let you go over to your friend's house, you would clean the kitchen before going to bed. You get home and you are just exhausted. What should you do?

1 Pass

You would really like to take a dance class. You are already on a soccer team. The dance classes are on the same nights as your soccer practices. What should you do?

3 Passes

Pretend like you are asking your mom if you can take a guitar class. Be sure to include details such as: the day the class meets, when it starts, and how much it costs.

2 Passes

Your mom says that you can only go to the movies if you do a good job of being responsible this week. What are five things you can do to show her that you can be responsible?

1 Pass

You would like to run faster. What should you do in order to reach this goal?

3 Passes

You would like to improve in art. What should you do in order to reach this goal?

2 Passes

You would like to learn how to dive and swim. What should you do in order to reach this goal?

1 Pass

You would like to learn how to do a flip. What should you do in order to reach this goal?

3 Passes

You told your friend that you would go over to her house on Saturday. On Friday night, you stay up late and are very tired on Saturday. You would rather stay in bed than go to her house. What should you do?

2 Passes

You told your friend that you would play football with him in the afternoon. However, after you get home, you just want to watch TV. You know that he is waiting for you. What should you do?

1 Pass

Dear Parents/Guardians,

Today, your child participated in a classroom guidance game entitled, "Responsible Soccer." The objective of this game was to emphasize the importance of responsible behaviors. We discussed ways that we can behave responsibly such as setting goals, using good study skills, and taking ownership of actions.

In this game, students competed against each other on teams. Players picked cards with questions about responsible, reliable behaviors. If correctly answered, teams were able to pass the soccer ball (on our soccer field game board) one to three times. Each time the ball reached the goal, the team scored a point.

At home tonight, you can praise your child for areas in which he/she behaves responsibly. You can point out the strengths that he/she has in this area.

Thanks for your support,

Game #46

Grade Levels
2-6

Materials
- Copy of Study Skills Draw Cards (pp.235-236)
- Markers
- Whiteboard or Paper

Time Needed
Approximately 30 minutes

Skills Covered
- Study Skills
- Goal Setting
- Responsibility

Study Skills Draw

Introduction
This game is a fun game that everyone loves. Students get to draw and practice responsible study skills!

Pre-Game Directions

1. Encourage students to brainstorm many different study skills.

2. Talk about the importance of using good study skills at home and at school. Ask students about study skills that help them be successful when doing homework, taking tests, and doing classwork.

3. Explain that we will be playing a game where teams compete by drawing and correctly guessing responsible study skills.

4. Divide the class into two teams.

5. Go over the rules –
   - You cannot write words or letters.
   - You cannot talk.

6. You will have one minute for your team to guess the main idea of your card.

7. If your team guesses correctly, your team will get one point.

8. Points will be deducted for students getting out of their seats or unsportsmanlike behaviors.

Game Directions

1. Player #1 from Team A picks a card from the pile.

2. Player #1 begins drawing pictures to describe the study skills described on the card.

3. Team A has one minute to guess what the player is depicting.

4. If Team A guesses the main idea of the card in less than one minute, Team A receives one point.

5. Team B proceeds as Team A.

6. Continue as time allows. Team with the most points wins.

Follow-Up

- Help class create a paper chain of study skills. Give each student three slips of paper. Instruct the students to write down three goals (one on each slip of paper) to help them improve their study skills. Make a chain from the slips of paper. Hang the chain in the classroom as a visual reminder to the class of their goals to improve their study skills.

Study Skills Draw Cards

Use a dictionary.

Sharpen your pencil before class begins.

Check your answers.

Color in the circle completely on a test.

Organize your desk.

Organize your backpack.

Get enough sleep.

Eat a good breakfast.

Wear comfortable clothing during a test.

Organize your paper before beginning to write.

Have someone quiz you.

Work with a study buddy.

Study Skills Draw Cards

Study in an area with good lighting.

Study in a quiet area.

Do your homework at a desk.

Ask your teacher questions if you do not understand.

Pay attention in class.

Be prepared for class.

Be quiet in class.

Use neat handwriting.

Have an extra pencil.

Make flashcards.

Don't wait until the night before a test to begin studying.

Plan ahead for a project.

Dear Parents/Guardians,

Today, your child participated in a classroom guidance game entitled, "Study Skills Draw." The objective of this game was to teach students the importance of using good study skills at school and at home. We talked about how tattling is usually used to get someone else in trouble. We discussed study skills that contribute to our success in homework, classwork, and on tests.

In this game, students were divided into two teams. Players picked cards with descriptions of study skills and attempted to silently draw these study skills for their teams. Points were awarded for correctly guessing the study skills on the cards.

At home tonight, you can talk to your child about his/her three best study skills. You can talk about how these skills help him/her succeed. Your child can also talk about his/her three weakest study skills and ways to improve them.

Thanks for your support,

Game #47

Grade Levels
2-6

Materials
- Copy of Top Five Question Cards (pg.240)
- Paper
- Pencils
- Tape

Time Needed
Approximately 30 minutes

Skills Covered
- Study Skills
- Goal Setting
- Responsibility

Top Five

Introduction

This is a fun game where teams compete against one another to correctly answer questions about study skills.

Pre-Game Directions

1. Copy and cut out Top Five Question Cards.

2. Explain to students that they will be participating in a classroom game about successful study skills. The class will be divided into four teams that will compete against one another.

3. Discuss study skills with the class. Ask the students about study skills that help them at home and at school. Encourage students to share study habits that have helped improve their grades (example, packing backpack the night before, doing homework shortly after arriving home). Talk about study habits that have a negative effect on grades (example, waiting until the last minute, not being prepared for school).

4. Explain that the teams will answer questions about study skills. Each question has five different answers ranking in points from 1-5. The teams must each make a list of seven answers. The teams will collect points for any answers that match the answers on the question card.

Game Directions

1. Divide the class into four teams. Instruct the teams to name themselves.

2. Ask a Top Five question to all teams. The teams will have three minutes to think of seven answers for the Top Five questions.

3. At the end of three minutes, collect the answers and have one of the team members read the answers aloud. Teams will collect points for any answers that match the answers on the question card.

4. Repeat steps #2 and #3.

5. Continue as time allows. Team with the most points wins.

Top Five

Follow-Up

- Describe the area in which you study at home. Describe the lighting, noises, seating, etc. Do you have all the supplies you need in your work area? Do you think your work area is a good place for you to do your homework? Please explain why.
- What do you think are the most important study skills to use at school? At home? Please explain why.
- What is your plan for completing homework? Do you begin it as soon as you get home? Which subject do you do first? Do you get help from someone at home? Do you put it in your bookbag when you finish? What homework skills are do you need to improve?

Grade Levels

2-6

Materials

- Copy of Top Five Question Cards (pg.240)
- Paper
- Pencils
- Tape

Time Needed

Approximately 30 minutes

Skills Covered

- Study Skills
- Goal Setting
- Responsibility

Top Five Question Cards

TOP FIVE
Things You Should Have in Your Backpack

- **Pencils** *(5 points)*
- **Paper** *(4 points)*
- **Notebooks** *(3 points)*
- **Books** *(2 points)*
- **Crayons** *(1 point)*

TOP FIVE
Tips for Studying for a Test

- **Read Your Notes** *(5 points)*
- **Study in a Quiet Area** *(4 points)*
- **Have a Parent Quiz You** *(3 points)*
- **Make Flashcards** *(2 points)*
- **Go To Bed Early** *(1 point)*

TOP FIVE
Tips for Bringing Up a Low Grade

- **Ask Your Teacher for Help** *(5 points)*
- **Do All Your Homework** *(4 points)*
- **Pay Attention in Class** *(3 points)*
- **Ask Your Parents for Help** *(2 points)*
- **Work With a Tutor or a Study Buddy** *(1 point)*

TOP FIVE
Tips for Writing a Paper

- **Organize It Before Writing** *(5 points)*
- **Write Down Your Ideas** *(4 points)*
- **Make a Rough Draft** *(3 points)*
- **Revise and Edit** *(2 points)*
- **Proofread Your Final Copy** *(1 point)*

TOP FIVE
Tips for Doing a Book Report

- **Read the Book** *(5 points)*
- **Include the Main Ideas** *(4 points)*
- **Include the Main Characters** *(3 points)*
- **Organize It Before Writing** *(2 points)*
- **Proofread Your Final Copy** *(1 point)*

TOP FIVE
Tips for Doing Well on a Test

- **Read the Entire Question** *(5 points)*
- **Read the Directions** *(4 points)*
- **Go to Bed Early** *(3 points)*
- **Have 2 Sharpened Pencils** *(2 points)*
- **Eat a Good Breakfast** *(1 point)*

TOP FIVE
Tips for Doing Your Homework

- **Begin Shortly After You Get Home** *(5 points)*
- **Have Everything You Need in One Place** *(4 points)*
- **Ask for Help if You Need It** *(3 points)*
- **Do Your Work in a Quiet Place** *(2 points)*
- **Do Your Work at a Desk or Table** *(1 point)*

TOP FIVE
Tips for Getting Good Grades

- **Do Your Homework** *(5 points)*
- **Pay Attention in Class** *(4 points)*
- **Study for Tests** *(3 points)*
- **Be Well-Prepared for Class** *(2 points)*
- **Ask Your Teacher for Help** *(1 point)*

TOP FIVE
Tips for Making a Good Study Area

- **Quiet Place** *(5 points)*
- **Good Lighting** *(4 points)*
- **Use of a Desk or Table** *(3 points)*
- **Away from Distractions** *(2 points)*
- **Well-Stocked With Study Supplies** *(1 point)*

TOP FIVE
Tips for Good Organization

- **Pack Your Backpack at Night** *(5 points)*
- **Put Everything in a Specific Place** *(4 points)*
- **Clean Out Your Backpack Once a Week** *(3 points)*
- **Clean Out Your Desk Once a Week** *(2 points)*
- **Make Sure You Have Everything You Need** *(1 point)*

Dear Parents/Guardians,

Today, your child participated in a classroom guidance game entitled, "Top Five." The objective of this game was to teach and review responsible behaviors at school and at home. We discussed good study skills such as packing your backpack the night before school. We also discussed poor study skills, such as waiting until the last minute to study for a test. We talked about the negative and positive effects these study skills can have on our school success.

In this game, students were divided into four teams. Players were asked to name the top five tips for specific areas of study skills (such as the top five tips for making a good study area). Teams received points for correct answers.

At home tonight, you can go over the "top five" requests that you have for your child to succeed at school.

Thanks for your support,

Game #48

Responsible Tic-Tac-Toe

Grade Levels

2-6

Materials

- Copy of Responsibility Tic-Tac-Toe Cards (pp.244-245)
- Whiteboard or Chalkboard
- Dry Erase Markers or Chalk
- Nine Envelopes

Time Needed

Approximately 30 minutes

Skills Covered

- Responsible Behaviors
- Goal Setting
- Achieving Goals

Introduction

This game is a wonderful way to teach and review organization, study skills, goal setting, and careers while engaging in a fun classroom game of tic-tac-toe.

Pre-Game Directions

1. Number each envelope #1 - #9.

2. Copy and cut out Responsibility Tic-Tac-Toe Cards.

3. Divide Responsibility Tic-Tac-Toe Cards evenly between nine envelopes.

4. Draw tic-tac-toe board on whiteboard or chalkboard.

5. Number each square on the tic-tac-toe board #1 - #9.

6. Talk to the students about the importance of responsibility. Talk about the importance of time management, organization, and planning. Talk about the importance of setting goals and making plans to achieve those goals.

7. Ask students to give examples of responsible behaviors if they want to get a good grade on a test. Ask students to give examples of future careers and ways that they can begin preparing for these careers now and in the future.

8. Explain to the students that they will be participating in a tic-tac-toe game where they will answer questions about responsible behaviors in order to place an "O" or an "X" on the board.

9. Explain that each square on the tic-tac-toe board has a number that matches an envelope. Teams will compete against one another (the X's and the O's) by taking turns answering questions about responsibility. In order to place a mark on the board, the team must choose the number of the square in which they wish to place a mark. The team member must then answer a question from an envelope that matches the number of that square on the tic-tac-toe board. If answered correctly, that team gets to put a mark in that box. Teams take turns until one team has three X's or three O's in a row.

Responsible Tic-Tac-Toe

Game Directions

1. Player from Team X picks a numbered square on the Tic-Tac-Toe Board and answers a question from the same numbered envelope. If correctly answered, Team X can place an X in the square. For example, if the player picks the #3 box on the Tic-Tac-Toe board, the player will pick a question from the #3 envelope. If correctly answered, the player can put a mark in the #3 box on the Tic-Tac-Toe board.

2. Player from Team O proceeds as Team X.

3. The first team to get three X's or three O's in a row gets one point.

4. Erase X's and O's.

5. Next game begins with Team X having first turn.

6. Continue as time allows. The team with most points wins.

Follow-Up

- What is a goal that you set and achieved? What techniques did you use to help you achieve this goal?
- What is a goal that you did not achieve? What do you think made this goal so difficult for you? How could you achieve this goal now?
- Name a goal that you would like to achieve. What are three steps that will help you achieve this goal?

Materials
- Copy of Responsibility Tic-Tac-Toe Cards (pp.244-245)
- Whiteboard or Chalkboard
- Dry Erase Markers or Chalk
- Nine Envelopes

Time Needed
Approximately 30 minutes

Skills Covered
- Responsible Behaviors
- Goal Setting
- Achieving Goals

Responsible Tic-Tac-Toe Cards

Give an example of a responsible schedule after arriving home from school.

What is the name of the job of a person who works in a school and helps people learn?

Name three careers that you could try to have if you are good at making things and using your hands.

Describe the job of a doctor. Where do doctors work? Do you have to be sick to go to a doctor? Why or why not?

Why is it important to be a good reader and writer? How can this help you in a future job?

If you get home from school at 4:00 and dinner is at 6:00, explain how you will have enough time to eat your snack, take a break, do your homework, and set the table.

If you want to make more baskets in basketball, what should you do to reach this goal?

Name three careers you could try to have if you are good at working with children.

If you are interested in being a firefighter when you grow up, what are some things you should do to help you achieve this goal?

If you want to be a better artist, name three things you should do in order to reach this goal.

What is the name of the job of a person who works in a restaurant and makes food?

Why is it important to learn math in school? How would you use math in a job? How do you use math at home? How do you use math at the store?

If you want to be a better football player, name three things you should do to help you reach this goal.

Name five things you should have in your backpack.

When your teacher gives you a paper to take home, explain how you will make sure that your parents get the paper.

Responsible Tic-Tac-Toe Cards

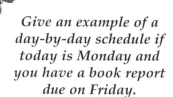 Give an example of a day-by-day schedule if today is Monday and you have a book report due on Friday.

 What is the name of the job of a person who helps clean up and take care of schools and other public areas?

 Give an example of a day-by day schedule if today is Monday and you have a test on Friday.

 Name five things that a good study area should include.

Name five ways to help improve your grades.

If you want to be a better friend and have more friends, what are three things you can do in order to reach this goal?

Name five things that a police officer does in his/her job.

 If you want to learn to play the guitar, what are some things you can do to help you reach this goal?

 Give an example of a day-by-day schedule if today is Monday and you have a science project due on Friday.

 Name a career that you would like to have and explain some things you will have to do in order to train for this job.

 If you need to catch the bus at 7:30, what time should you wake up? How will you make sure you get up at this time? What time should you go to bed?

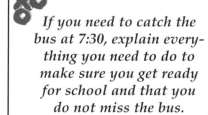 If you need to catch the bus at 7:30, explain everything you need to do to make sure you get ready for school and that you do not miss the bus.

 If you want to be well-prepared and on time for school on Tuesday, explain everything you need to do on Monday.

 If you love music and are interested in having a career in music, what are some things you can do now and in the future to help you have a career in music?

 Name three kind of careers you could have in music.

Dear Parents/Guardians,

Today, your child participated in a classroom guidance game entitled, "Responsibility Tic-Tac-Toe." The objective of this game was to teach students the importance of responsible behaviors such as time management, setting goals, organization, and planning. We discussed examples of responsible behaviors in order to get good grades and examples of planning for future goals and careers.

In this game, the class was divided into two teams – the X's and the O's. Teams competed by taking turns answering questions about responsibility. If correctly answered, teams were able to place X's or O's on the board.

At home tonight, you can encourage your child to talk about his/her goals and wishes for the future. You can help your child plan ways to achieve these goals.

Thanks for your support,

Get Rich

Game #49

Grade Levels
2-6

Materials
- 2 Copies of Get Rich Cards (pp.249-251)
- 1 Copy of Get Rich Elimination Cards (pg.252)
- 10 Copies of Get Rich Money (pg.253)
- Pencils for Each Team
- Paper for Each Team

Time Needed
Approximately 30 minutes

Skills Covered
- Careers
- Study Skills
- Goal Setting
- Responsibility

Introduction
This game is a fun way to teach study skills, career information, organizational skills, time management and responsibility.

Pre-Game Directions

1. Copy and cut out Get Rich Cards, Money, and Elimination Cards.

2. Explain to class that they will be participating in a game where teams compete against each other for fun money by answering questions about study skills, career information, organizational skills, time management, and responsibility. Talk to students about the importance of engaging in responsible behaviors that will contribute to the success of their grades, their conduct, and their future careers.

3. Explain that questions will increase in difficulty as they increase in money.

4. Explain that the class will be divided into two teams. Teams will compete against each other for fun money. Each team will have four opportunities for an answer to be eliminated from their Get Rich Card in order to provide assistance in answering the question. Each time one answer is eliminated, one elimination card is used. More than one elimination card can be used to eliminate more than one answer on a single card. If a team answers a question incorrectly, the opposing team is given $500 and both teams must start over again with the $100 dollar question.

Game Directions

1. Class is divided into two teams – A and B.

2. Each team is given four elimination cards. Each card may only be used ONCE. However, more than one elimination card can be used in answering one question. If a question is incorrectly answered, the opposing team will be given $500 and both teams will begin again with another $100 question.

3. The game begins with one player from Team A and one player from Team B answering one of the $100 questions. The players are each given the question card to look at and they must each write down their answers on a piece of paper and turn it in. If answered correctly, teams get $100.

Game #49

Grade Levels

2-6

Materials

• 2 Copies of Get Rich Cards (pp.249-251)

• 1 Copy of Get Rich Elimination Cards (pg.252)

• 10 Copies of Get Rich Money (pg.253)

• Pencils for Each Team

• Paper for Each Team

Time Needed

Approximately 30 minutes

Skills Covered

• Careers

• Study Skills

• Goal Setting

• Responsibility

Get Rich

Game Directions continued...

4. If a player needs assistance with a question, he/she may turn in and use an elimination card after the opposing team has written down its answer. When using an elimination card, the teacher / counselor will cross out one of the answers on the question card in order to help the player answer the question. Each team is given only four elimination cards for the entirety of the game. More than one elimination card can be used on one question, or the elimination cards can be used on different questions.

5. After $100 questions are asked and correctly answered, the next player from each team will be asked a $200 question. If correctly answered, teams will get $200 and will next be asked the $300 questions.

6. Play as time allows. Team with the most points wins the game.

Follow-Up

• What is your biggest strength in organization? What is your biggest weakness in organization?
• What is your biggest strength in planning and goal setting? What is your biggest weakness in planning and goal setting?
• What is your biggest strength in study skills? What is your biggest weakness in study skills?

Get Rich Cards

$100 $100 $100 $100 $100 $100 $100

Which of the following is an example of good study skills?

A) Studying at a desk
B) Studying outside
C) Studying in front of the television
D) Not studying at all

$100 $100 $100 $100 $100 $100 $100

Which of the following is an example of poor study skills?

A) Studying in a well-lit area
B) Studying in a place where your study materials are available
C) Studying in your bed
D) Studying in an area with very few distractions

$100 $100 $100 $100 $100 $100 $100

Which of the following is an example of a well-organized backpack?

A) A neat and orderly backpack that contains pencils, paper, notebooks, and textbooks
B) A backpack that has papers sticking out of it and old candy wrappers falling out of it
C) A backpack that has broken pencils, ripped papers and notebooks, and broken crayons
D) A backpack that has a broken zipper and broken armstraps

$100 $100 $100 $100 $100 $100 $100

Which of the following is an example of poor test preparation?

A) Staying up all night the night before a test
B) Having a good breakfast the morning of a test
C) Wearing comfortable clothing to school on the day of a test
D) Reviewing your notes before beginning a test

$100 $100 $100 $100 $100 $100 $100

Which of the following is an example of good test taking skills?

A) Circling the first answer you see for each question
B) Only reading the directions that are short sentences
C) Reading the whole question and all answers before answering the question
D) Finishing as quickly as possible

$100 $100 $100 $100 $100 $100 $100

Which of the following is an example of good classroom behavior:

A) Tipping your desk backwards
B) Paying attention to your teacher
C) Writing notes to your friends
D) Throwing paper airplanes

$100 $100 $100 $100 $100 $100 $100

Which of the following jobs helps put out fires?

A) Fireman
B) Mailman
C) Dentist
D) Policeman

$100 $100 $100 $100 $100 $100 $100

Which of the following jobs works with people's teeth?

A) Doctor
B) Florist
C) Cardiologist
D) Dentist

$200 $200 $200 $200 $200 $200 $200

Which of the following jobs works with wood?

A) Photographer
B) Carpenter
C) Mechanic
D) Artist

$200 $200 $200 $200 $200 $200 $200

Pick the **BEST** answer.
Which of the following answers is a job that helps people learn Math?

A) Secretary
B) Teacher
C) Principal
D) Counselor

Get Rich Cards

$200 $200 $200 $200 $200 $200 $200

Pick the **BEST** answer.

Which of the following answers is a job that helps protect people?

A) Teacher
B) Karate Teacher
C) Police Officer
D) Pastor

$200 $200 $200 $200 $200 $200 $200

Pick the **BEST** answer.

Which of the following answers is a job where someone works using their hands to create things?

A) Doctor
B) Waiter/Waitress
C) Artist
D) Dog Trainer

$200 $200 $200 $200 $200 $200 $200

Which of the following words is spelled correctly?

A) Libary
B) Libraray
C) Library
D) Liberry

$200 $200 $200 $200 $200 $200 $200

Which of the following words is spelled correctly?

A) Responsibility
B) Ressponsbility
C) Responsybylity
D) Responzibillity

$300 $300 $300 $300 $300 $300 $300

Which of the following words is spelled correctly?

A) Organization
B) Orrganizzation
C) Organnizzation
D) Orrgannizzattion

$300 $300 $300 $300 $300 $300 $300

Which of the following is the first thing you should do when taking a test?

A) Read the questions
B) Read the directions
C) Answer the questions
D) Read all answers

$300 $300 $300 $300 $300 $300 $300

Which of the following is something you can do the night before in order to help you get ready for school in the morning?

A) Get dressed
B) Eat breakfast
C) Pick out your clothes
D) Ride the bus

$300 $300 $300 $300 $300 $300 $300

Which of the following is something you can do to improve your organization?

A) Study for tests
B) Do your homework
C) Clean out your backpack
D) Keep your eyes on your own paper

$300 $300 $300 $300 $300 $300 $300

Which of the following is spelled correctly?

A) Dictionary
B) Spell Cheker
C) Thesarus
D) Computur

$300 $300 $300 $300 $300 $300 $300

Which of the following is spelled correctly?

A) Notbook
B) Pensils
C) Crayonns
D) Ruler

Get Rich Cards

$400 $400 $400 $400 $400 $400 $400

Which of the following is spelled correctly?

A) Journal
B) Texbook
C) Noval
D) Ajenda

$400 $400 $400 $400 $400 $400 $400

Where does an anchorman/woman usually work?

A) Computer Lab
B) Television Station
C) Navy Ship
D) Art Studio

$400 $400 $400 $400 $400 $400 $400

What does a receptionist usually do at his/her job?

A) Decorate homes
B) Answer phones and make appointments
C) Recycle newspapers
D) Arrange flowers

$400 $400 $400 $400 $400 $400 $400

What does a taxidermist usually do at his/her job?

A) Files people's taxes
B) Works with money management and banking
C) Stuffs animals (that are dead) for display
D) Hunts wild animals

$400 $400 $400 $400 $400 $400 $400

Which of the following words is spelled incorrectly?

A) Excavator
B) Principal
C) Lawyer
D) Custodion

$500 $500 $500 $500 $500 $500 $500

Which of the following words is spelled incorrectly?

A) Paramedic
B) Anesthesiologist
C) Computer Technicion
D) Chemical Engineer

$500 $500 $500 $500 $500 $500 $500

Which of the following words is spelled incorrectly?

A) Biologist
B) Arborist
C) Flourist
D) Electrician

$500 $500 $500 $500 $500 $500 $500

Which of the following words is spelled correctly?

A) Geolagist
B) Ophthalmologist
C) Orthoadontist
D) Podyatrist

$500 $500 $500 $500 $500 $500 $500

Which of the following words is spelled correctly?

A) Paleontologist
B) Zooloogist
C) Archaeolagist
D) Cardiolagist

$500 $500 $500 $500 $500 $500 $500

Which of the following words is spelled correctly?

A) Pharmocist
B) Archatect
C) Oceanographer
D) Chemmist

Get Rich Money

Dear Parents/Guardians,

Today, your child participated in a classroom guidance game entitled, "Get Rich." The objective of this game was to teach and review study skills, career information, organizational skills, time management and responsibility. We discussed the importance of engaging in behaviors that positively contribute to our grades, our conduct, and our futures.

In this game, the class was divided into two teams. Teams competed for "money" by correctly answering questions about responsible behaviors.

At home tonight, you can help your child clean out and organize his/her backpack. Sometimes it takes someone else's assistance to get us on the right track.

Thanks for your support,

Career Bowling

Grade Levels

2-6

Materials

- Copy of Career Bowling Questions (pp.257-259)
- 10 Empty Plastic Bottles
- Ball
- Envelope
- Masking Tape

Time Needed

Approximately 30 minutes

Skills Covered

- Career Information and Exploration
- Goal Setting

Introduction

Students will be introduced to different careers by playing a fun game of classroom bowling!

Pre-Game Directions

1. Copy and cut apart career questions.

2. Put career questions in an envelope.

3. Set up empty plastic soda bottles as bowling pins in front of classroom.

4. Mark space with tape where student is to stand when bowling.

5. Explain to class that they will be participating in a game where teams will compete to correctly answer questions about careers in order to have opportunities to "bowl" in the classroom!

6. Explain to students that all questions in the bowling game will be focused on career information.

7. Ask students to talk about jobs they would like to have as adults. Discuss the types of training and education these jobs will require.

8. Talk about decisions that students can make now that will help them in future careers. For example, it is important to attend school every day and to work hard in all subjects so that they will have many choices of future training and education. Students need to set goals for themselves.

Game Directions

1. Divide class into two teams.

2. First player from Team A rolls ball into bowling pins. If the player misses and does not knock down any pins, the player gets another chance to bowl.

3. If the player knocks down any pins, he/she must then pick a question from the envelope.

4. The player reads and answers the career question. If correctly answered, the team gets the same number of points as the number of knocked down pins, unless the player picks a WILD card.

Game #50

Grade Levels

2-6

Materials

- Copy of Career Bowling Questions (pp.257-259)
- 10 Empty Plastic Bottles
- Ball
- Envelope
- Masking Tape

Time Needed

Approximately 30 minutes

Skills Covered

- Career Information and Exploration
- Goal Setting

Career Bowling

Game Directions continued...

5. If the player picks a WILD card (worth 10 points), he/she must answer these questions:

   What career interests you?

   What kind of education or training will you need for this career?

6. Team B proceeds as Team A.

7. Game continues as time allows. The team with the most points wins the game.

Follow-Up

- Interview three people who have careers in your community.
- Ask the following questions to the people you interview:

   What is your full name?

   What is the name of your job?

   Where do you work?

   What type of environment do you work in? (Outside, inside, loud, quiet, etc.)

   What type of education and training helped you get this job?

   Describe a typical day at your job.

   What job did you aspire to when you were a child?

   How did you decide to work in your career area?

   What are your favorite things about your job?

   What are your least favorite things about your job?

- Present the three interviews to your class.

Career Bowling Questions

 This job is in education and helps children learn.
This person is called a _____.

 This person wears a blue uniform and protects people. This person drives a car or a motorcycle to help enforce laws.
This person is called a _____.

 This person is in charge of a school.
This person is a _____.

 This person works in schools and community agencies. People talk to this person about their problems.
This person is a _____.

 If you are sick, your mom takes you to this person. This person examines you and finds out what is wrong with you and how to help make you better.
This person is a _____.

 This person often helps a doctor. You may also have one of these at your school. He/she usually takes your temperature, weighs you, and helps you look at the eye chart.
The name of this job is a _____.

 This person rides in a red truck and helps put out fires.
The name of this job is a _____.

 This person transports items from one part of the country to another. This person may transport items such as: drinks, machinery, food, lumber, etc. This person spends a lot of time "on the road."
This person is called a _____.

 People call this person if they want to change the color of their house from brown to white.
This person is called a _____.

 This person raises animals and food to sell to stores and to people. This person lives in the country.
This person is called a _____.

 This person examines your teeth and fixes cavities.
This person is called a _____.

 This person works in an office. This person answers phones, works on the computer, files papers, and helps people. This person is called a/an:
a) orthodontist   b) pharmacist   c) secretary

 This person helps fix computers. This person is called a:
a) computer person   b) computer salesperson   c) computer technician

Career Bowling Questions

 You call this person if you need help fixing your sink, pipes, or your shower.
This person is called a _____.

 If you need braces, you go see this person:
a) orthodontist   b) teethdontist   c) bracesdontist

 You take your pets to this kind of doctor:
a) veterinarian   b) veterologist   c) vetographer

 This person takes your order in a restaurant. This person brings the food to your table.
This person is called a _____.

 This person works with metal. He/she applies heat to metal and joins pieces of metal together. This person is called a:
a) metalographer   b) welder   c) melter

 This person is in charge of a team of athletes. This person teaches this team how to play the sport and helps them win games.
This person is called a _____.

 This person drives a big yellow vehicle to school with lots of students in it.
This person is called a _____.

 This person manages money according to the stock market. This person is called a:
a) stock broker   b) stock driver   c) stock manager

 This person brings you food and drinks on an airplane.
This person is called a _____.

 This person flies an airplane.
He/she is called a _____.

 How much education do you need to be an elementary school teacher?
a) High School Diploma   b) 4-year College Degree   c) 2-year College Associate's Degree

This person advises people about what their rights are under the law. People might hire this person if they are going to court. This person is called a:
a) judge   b) lawyer   c) accountant

 This person works with money management. People might hire this person to help with their taxes. This person is called a:
a) lawyer   b) accountant   c) manager

Career Bowling Questions

 This person studies the ocean. This person is called a:

   a) geologist   b) diver   c) oceanographer

 This person helps keep stores and other private properties safe. This person wears a uniform. This person is called a:

   a) firefighter   b) security guard   c) protector

 This person does research and experiments in order to help find answers to problems. This person is called a:

   a) scientist   b) chiropractor   c) instructor

 This person is a doctor who works with your eyes. This person is called a:

   a) podiatrist   b) opthamologist   c) pharmacist

 You go to this person to get prescriptions filled for medicine:

   a) pharmacist   b) prescriptioner   c) medicine man

 This person helps clean and care for buildings. This person is called a:

   a) cleaner   b) custodian   c) caregiver

 This person explores, studies, and even travels to space. This person is called an:

   a) architect   b) astronomer   c) astronaut

 ## WILD CARD - 10 POINTS
• What career interests you?   • What kind of education or training will you need for this career?

 ## WILD CARD - 10 POINTS
• What career interests you?   • What kind of education or training will you need for this career?

 ## WILD CARD - 10 POINTS
• What career interests you?   • What kind of education or training will you need for this career?

 ## WILD CARD - 10 POINTS
• What career interests you?   • What kind of education or training will you need for this career?

 ## WILD CARD - 10 POINTS
• What career interests you?   • What kind of education or training will you need for this career?

 ## WILD CARD - 10 POINTS
• What career interests you?   • What kind of education or training will you need for this career?

Dear Parents/Guardians,

Today, your child participated in a classroom guidance game entitled, "Career Bowling." The objective of this game was to teach and review career information. Students discussed their interest in different careers. We talked about the training and education required for various careers.

In this game, the class was divided into two teams. Players participated in a game of bowling – rolling a small ball into a set of ten plastic bottles. Teams earned points for the number of bottles knocked down after players correctly answered questions about careers.

At home tonight, you can talk to your child about a workplace that he/she would like to visit. Your child may be able to visit you or a family member at work and learn more about the workplace.

Thanks for your support,

About the Author

Shannon Trice Black is a Licensed Professional Counselor and an Elementary School Counselor in Goochland, Virginia. She works in the same school system in which she was a student! She earned a Master's Degree of Counselor Education from the University of Virginia and Bachelor of Art Degrees in Psychology and English from the College of William and Mary. She lives in Virginia with her two daughters and her husband, Gary, who is also an educator. She loves to read, run, do yoga, and spend time with friends and family.

Shannon is pictured below with students from Byrd Elementary School where she is a school counselor.

Pictured from left to right are Tyler Ott, Jamie Bell, Romeka Coles, Shannon Trice Black, Madelyn Ott, Aniya Hope, and Rondell Coles.